Natural Church Development and Cell Church - Friends or Foes?

NATURAL CHURCH DEVELOPMENT AND CELL CHURCH - FRIENDS OR FOES?

LESLIE H. BRICKMAN, D.MIN
Professor of Cell Church at Regent University

Copyright © 2005 by Leslie H. Brickman

Natural Church Development and Cell Church
by Leslie H. Brickman

Printed in the United States of America

ISBN 1-594679-20-7

All rights reserved solely by the author. The author guarantees all contents are original and do not infringe upon the legal rights of any other person or work. No part of this book may be reproduced in any form without the permission of the author. The views expressed in this book are not necessarily those of the publisher.

Unless otherwise indicated, Bible quotations are taken from the New American Standard Bible, The Open Bible Addition. Copyright © 1978, 1979, by Thomas Nelson Publishers. Copyright © 1960, 1962, 1963, 1971, 1972, 1973, 1975, 1977 by The Lockman Foundation.

www.xulonpress.com

Psalm 133

Behold, how good and how pleasant it is
For brothers to dwell together in unity!

It is like the precious oil upon the head,
Coming down upon the beard,
Even Aaron's beard,
Coming down upon the edge of his robes.

It is like the dew of Hermon
Coming down upon the mountains of Zion;
For there the LORD commanded the blessing—
life forever.

This work is dedicated to two instruments of the Lord:

Paul Jeong, who planted the first seed, and

Twyla Brickman, my life partner in ministry,
who nourished, cultivated, and
labored to see the fruit come forth.

CONTENTS

Introduction..ix

Chapter 1 - A Journey of Discovery...1
  Discovering Small Groups...2
  Discovering Cell Groups...4
  Discovering Natural Church Development..5

Chapter 2 - A Bird's Eye View of NCD.......................................7
  What is Natural Church Development?..11
  Origins and Continuing Research..13
  Building Block #1: Eight Quality Characteristics.............................14
  Building Block #2: Six Biotic Principles..16
  Building Block #3: Minimum Strategy..26
  Bipolar Ecclesiology..27

Chapter 3 - Releasing Stereophonic Cell Ministry............31
Viewing Edification Through Bipolar Lenses...................32
Dynamic Partnership - Jesus and Me..............................37
Divine Revelation - Dealing with Roots Not Fruits 49
Decisive Transformation - When is a Door not a Door?...52
Deliberate Renovation - Re-building by A Divine Plumbline...........53
Lasting Edification 54

Chapter 4 - Growing Stereophonic Cell Churches.................57
The Bipolar Nature of the Church - Ephesian Ecclesiology...........58
The Problem with Cells & Celebration.............................62
Developing a Values-Driven Organic Operating System...................69
An Organic Operating Model - Spiritual Body Systems.....................79
Implications..117

Chapter 5 - Learning to Think & Plan Biotically..............121
Transitioning Small Groups to Cells.................................122
Case Study - Riverside Community Church.....................124
Processing A Possible Solution - Learning to Think Biotically........132
Conclusions 150

Chapter 6 - Learning to Evaluate Biotically.......................153
The Challenge Before Us...154
In the Beginning...155
Life Happens..161
And It Came to Pass..163
Learning to Release the "What Might Have Been".........166

Chapter 7 - Your Next Step..171

INTRODUCTION

BUT BEYOND THIS, MY SON, BE WARNED: THE WRITING OF MANY BOOKS IS ENDLESS, AND EXCESSIVE DEVOTION TO BOOKS IS WEARYING TO THE BODY.
ECCLESIASTES. 12:12

Introduction

CONCEIVED IN THE HEART OF SEOUL

Have you ever picked up a book and asked yourself, "How did the author come to write this? How did this book actually come about?" I have. You may wonder about the book you now hold in your hands. So, let me begin with a story...

It was November of 2002. I was teaching a Doctor of Ministry course at Regent University entitled *Birthing the Cell Church*, when a representative from the D.Min. office abruptly came in and handed me a note. The note was an urgent request to travel to Seoul, Korea and teach a cell course, in two weeks! It seems that the designated professor had become violently ill. It was not until later that I would come to learn that the other speaker was a dear friend who had contracted malaria. Bill Beckham that week was fighting for his very life. One week later I was winging my way to Seoul Korea.

This was one of those acts of Divine Providence that you come to understand and appreciate only in retrospect. My host for the week was both a student and business entrepreneur, Paul Jeong. Paul heads up two organizations in the Republic of Korea, NCDKorea and TOUCHKorea. The first encourages Natural Church Development, while the second deals with the principles of cell church. As the teaching progressed throughout the week Paul alerted me that there was not only a chasm between those churches using NCD and cell churches, there was even an antagonism. Like me, Paul saw a great compatibility between the principles of cell church and Natural Church Development. Out of those series of conversations was born the desire to write a book helping to bridge that gap and quell the open antagonism. However, were these experiences unique to Korean churches? An unscheduled follow-on conversation three months later with Dr. Ralph Neighbour, wherein he detailed the problems elsewhere of a significant "cell" pastor who became involved with NCD and turned against cell churches, unfortunately confirmed what Paul had experienced.

A MEXICAN STANDOFF...

The principles of NCD and cell church are not mutually exclusive! It is not an "either, or" Mexican standoff. The issue should not be whether the church will employ NCD principles or be a cell church! The principles of both NCD and cell, far from being antithetical, can be mutually complimentary.

Can you be a cell church, not proactively employ the principles of NCD, and still experience health and growth? Yes. Health is a matter of degree. I can be healthy and eat few vegetables and fruit. I can be healthy and not drink two liters of water a day. I can be healthy and not be on an exercise regimen. However, I can be healthier if I do the aforementioned. I would suggest the principles of NCD when applied in a cell church context adds significantly to the overall health of the cell church.

Can a church that has chosen not to employ a cell based design and simply is using the principles of NCD still experience health and growth? Sure it can. Can a church using NCD have good holistic small groups that are not cells? Of course! There are many examples of such growing healthy churches today that are not cell based. However, the cell based design brings to the church a dimension and potential, which, in this author's opinion, will ultimately far outstrip that of a non-cell based design church.

Every church, cell and non-cell, is faced with five basic questions. How can we build up the Body of Christ? How can we most effectively disciple our people? From where will we get our future leaders? How can we reach this generation for Christ? How can we release our members into their God called and Spirit gifted ministries in the corporate church? These are the issues of edification, equipping, empowering, evangelism, and every member ministry. To non-cell based churches employing the principles of NCD, I would suggest that the cell based design provides the most effective wineskin for excelling at answering these questions.

...OR A SYMBIOTIC RELATIONSHIP?

Am I sold on NCD? Absolutely! Am I sold on cell church? Just as much. Do I think NCD and cell church can live and work together in a symbiotic relationship? Without a doubt. Toward this end has this book been written.

Chapter one will draw the reader into my own journey in search of community, cell church, and NCD. Chapter two will provide a bird's eye view of NCD. For the reader already familiar with NCD, it will provide a refresher. For the reader not yet acquainted, it will provide a brief overview of the salient features of Natural Church Development.

Introduction

Chapter three addresses the release of what I have called stereophonic cell ministry. The reader will be exposed to the benefits of cell edification implemented from an NCD bi-polar perspective. For those within the cell church movement, chapter four will perhaps pose the biggest challenge. It addresses the growing of stereophonic cell churches. The cell reader will be challenged to re-examine the cell church ecclesiology regarding the large group wing. I am afraid that we in the cell church movement are flying not with two wings, but with one and one-half wings.

Chapters five and six provide real life examples for the reader of how to apply NCD principles to cell church problems. The reader will be challenged to learn, to think, to plan and to evaluate biotically in a cell church context. Riverside Community Church in Nutley, New Jersey will provide the context for our examination. Riverside is a Christian and Missionary Alliance Church presently in transition to a cell based paradigm and implementing the principles of NCD. The final chapter will both look back in review from where we have come and forward toward where our next steps should lead us.

It is my observation that churches engaged in the process of Natural Church Development have come to the place of desiring greater health and more abundant fruit. They have that inner desire to become all that God has created them to be and to release the full abundance of life that the Head of the church has already placed within His Body. In like manner, I know that cell churches have a desire to once again experience the life and power of Christ so evident in the New Testament church and so necessary today if the Kingdom of God is to be established in the earth. They have chosen to embrace a new, yet old, paradigm for their wineskin to better facilitate and release this life of Christ. It seems to this author that in the final analysis, both groups are desiring similar things and are possessing different pieces of the puzzle.

The situation reminds me of the old story about the three blind men who ran into an elephant and were attempting to describe what it looked like, each from their own perspective. The blind man who had grabbed the swinging trunk had one perspective. The blind man who had bumped into the massive leg had another. The blind man holding the tail had a third. All were right. Yet, each needed the other's experience.

I would suggest that the perspective NCD brings to the church and the perspective brought by the cell church movement may, as in the illustration of the elephant, be combined to create a much fuller picture of that which Christ has created and how He desires His Body to function. That His Body may better prosper and grow, I commit this book into the reader's hands

Leslie H. Brickman
1 Mount Vernon Avenue
1st Floor
Bloomfield, NJ 07003

1

A Journey of Discovery

Now the Lord said to Abram,
"Go forth from your country,
and from your relatives
and from your father's house,
to the land which I will show you;
Genesis 12:1

Chapter 1 ✏ *A Journey of Discovery*

Growing up as a Jewish boy in the 1950's meant growing up with a built-in sense of community. It was no coincidence back then that Jewish children spent a considerable amount of recreation time at a place called the Jewish *Community* Center. It was, after all, a center for the Jewish community to congregate. Neither is it coincidence that Synagogue means assembly, and many synagogues are known as *Congregation* This-or-That. We always spoke about the Jewish *community* in Tucson, as if it was a monolithic community of Jews. The significance of becoming a Bar Mitzvah at thirteen, a Son of the Commandment, is that the Jewish boy now assumes full responsibility for his own sins and life as a full fledged member of the Jewish community. He is now able to become part of a minyon, sit shiva at funerals, and for all practical purposes serve as a member of the Jewish community. Marriage outside the faith weakens the community. Conversion to Christianity is anathema because it is as if a part of Israel has died. Growing up, the concept of community was never foreign and a sense of community was always a part of me.

In 1969 Jesus broke through my intense antagonism and religious pride and gloriously revealed Himself to me as my Messiah. I was suddenly born into His Kingdom and became a member of His family, the community of faith. I found out very quickly, however, that the Americanized church knew little about community, and practiced even less.

DISCOVERING SMALL GROUPS

Looking for Community

Becoming a member of the community of faith by no means meant I was experiencing what God intended as community. I discovered in the church a level of community far less than what I experienced as a Jew growing up in a secularized society. The practice of the church was far from that described within the pages of the New Testament. I was naive enough to believe from the outset that we were somehow to experience exactly what the Bible described. Thus began what would become a lifelong pursuit for an experience of New Testament community.

With the desire for community on the one hand, and the absence of true community in the church on the other hand, I was ripe for what was to follow. I spent a little over four of my early Christian years (1973-1977) as part of a church-turned-cult. To be sure, it possessed *community*, but a warped sense of the real thing. It offered a counterfeit community with a high price tag. It was in that context, though, that I began to discover the impact small groups of people could exert, for good or for evil.

After four years, having been delivered by the grace of God from the false, I continued my quest for the genuine. Having moved to Garland, Texas, I was again a part of a mainline denominational church that was experiencing little to no genuine community. Within short order, I found myself leading a small group of believers who were also on a similar quest. That year forged strong healthy relational ties. As we met week to week, we shared both the joys of our lives as well as the frustrations. However, that experience also was to be interrupted by a move, this time to Florida.

I soon began to experience a more genuine loving community within the context of another mainline denominational, though cutting edge, church in Tequesta, Florida. Maybe it was because a number of us were hungry for significant relationships. Maybe it was because we found a safe place to be real. For whatever reasons, a number of us bonded with a sense of genuine community. Some of those relationships continue and have now spanned more than two decades. That experience only served to whet my appetite for more.

I eventually planted a house church in our city in Florida. *Believers' Bible Fellowship*, by its very nature, was a small group. Through that church experience, God revealed many of the dynamics so essential to building Christian community, and many of the pitfalls along the way. It was to be three years later, however, that my experience with community via small groups would significantly deepen. While in seminary in Ft. Worth, Texas, I belonged to a church whose Senior Pastor was a former missionary, having worked with Pastor Dion Robert in Cote D'Ivoire. Jim Lassiter's desire was to see the dynamic experience of the mission field translated to the local church in America.

Discovering EFM and Kinship Groups

While completing my M.Div. at Southwestern Baptist Theological Seminary in Fort Worth, Texas, I was fortunate enough to be given the oppor-

Chapter 1 → A Journey of Discovery

tunity to lead one of the church's many *Extended Family Ministry Groups*, nicknamed EFMs. The initial pattern was borrowed from an Episcopalian church in Dallas. The emphasis of each EFM group was to build a sense of community through mutual edification. That was the normal small group emphasis in the US during the mid 1980s. Once again, the small group I led succeeded beyond my expectations and friendships have lasted nearly twenty years.

Soon after graduating from SWBTS in 1986, I was called to a church in Grand Forks, North Dakota. The church desired to experience small group life and "go on with the things of the Spirit." By this time the Vineyard movement was gaining momentum and we developed Kinship groups according to the small group pattern of the Vineyard. As we reached out to the community in which we lived, we were struck with the extremely high level of community already present in North Dakota. The lost culture around us had a higher level of community than we had ever experienced in the church!

As we attempted to evangelize those around us, we came to understand that we were not simply asking individuals for a commitment to Christ. They, for their part, were not struggling simply with whether or not to receive Christ. To receive Christ in an evangelical context was to say their religious upbringing and commitment was inadequate. This would lead to ostracism on the part of their community. As a consequence, they were really asking the question, "If I make a decision and am forced to leave my community, will you take care of me like they did?" The Lord sent us a prophetic word regarding our evangelism at this point. He said, "When the level of your community exceeds the level of their community, they will listen to you." It was here that the Lord led to the next discovery, cell groups.

DISCOVERING CELL GROUPS

There comes into your hands from time to time books that change you forever. Such a book was *Where Do We Go From Here?*, by Dr. Ralph Neighbour, Jr. That booked launched me into the cell church movement back in the late 1980's. That book became the "bible" for our cell group development, at least for awhile, at Faith Community Church in North Dakota. It put into concrete workable terms what I had merely dreamed of for many years, but did not understand how to achieve. Around the same time, a relationship began to develop between me and the staff at TOUCH Outreach Ministries in Houston, Texas. They were, after all, the "gurus" back then in cell church development. That relationship was to deepen as I joined the staff and a handful of other pastors from the U.S. for the First International Cell Church Conference at Faith Community Baptist Church in Singapore. What I saw in Singapore was what I had envisioned, and then some. I returned even more convinced that I was to transition the church where I served to the cell paradigm

The following year, I scheduled a cell conference with Bill Beckham. I had met Bill's son, Joey, on the trip to Singapore. At the time, Joey was heading up TOUCH Outreach Ministries in the United States. Bill's time with the church both solidified our transition and propelled us to the next level. In the fall of 1995, Dion Robert spent a week with us doing additional teaching and vision casting. Dion's own church at that time was well over 50,000. For all practical purposes we completed our transition to a cell church in 1995. It was soon after this that I felt impressed of the Lord to move to Texas to support Bill's attempt to plant a cell church in the Houston area. It was as a member of Shepherd Community that I came into relationship with Dr. Ralph Neighbour, Jr. Within the year, both my wife and I came on staff at TOUCH Outreach Ministries, Twyla ultimately developing the conference department, while I became involved in the development of *The Year of Transition* and pastoral consultation. As a result of my relationship with TOUCH, I also began what has continued to be a vibrant relationship with Regent University as an adjunct professor teaching the cell church curriculum.

DISCOVERING NATURAL CHURCH DEVELOPMENT

It was while working for TOUCH Outreach Ministries that I first learned about Natural Church Development. Christian Schwartz's book was newly published and the Board of TOUCH gave each employee a copy. The principles resonated with my own spirit. As I both continued to teach at Regent University and expand the teaching into Russia, I began to experiment and incorporate the NCD principles, as best I understood them, into the cell church development paradigm. Over the course of time I also felt the need to become an NCD coach. What has come out of that additional training and experience is an even greater appreciation and vision of how the biotic principles can be applied to every facet of cell church development.

Chapter 1 ☛ *A Journey of Discovery*

NCD AND CELL CHURCH - FRIENDS OR FOES?

For too long, I have perceived either an antagonistic stance, or at best, an ambivalent stance, by those of us within the cell movement toward NCD, and vise versa. While we may not be ready for a marriage, my hope is that we can enter into a symbiotic relationship and at least be friends. Chapter 2 provides a brief overview of the NCD concepts from which to proceed.

Christian Schwartz' concept of bipolarity poses a significant challenge for us when applied to our understanding of ecclesiology. In light of this concept, I would challenge us within the cell movement to re-examine our very concept regarding the nature of cell church. In our zeal, have we overcompensated for errors of the past and swung the pendulum too far? Chapters 3 and 4 are an attempt to view the issues of edification and the relationship of the cell to the corporate church body through this bipolar lens.

The mere fact that cell churches have holistic cell groups, even exceptionally holistic cell groups at times, in no way exempts us from the need to think biotically and practice the biotic principles in decision making. What a difference it would make if we both ran our decisions through the two-sided filter of cell paradigm and NCD paradigm, and asked the questions, "Is this good cell practice?" along with, "Is this decision biotic, that is, will it lead to 'all by itself growth'?" Chapters 5-7 are presented as a challenge to begin to think biotically and learn to also make cell decisions in accordance with biotic principles. Toward this end I have attempted to supply abundant examples of how this can be accomplished in a cell church environment. Are the examples flawless? Hardly. Is the thinking complete in every detail? Not at all. But, they have been developed in the trenches of an actual transitioning church, Riverside Community Church in Nutley, New Jersey. Riverside has chosen both to transition to a cell paradigm and to simultaneously embrace and apply the NCD principles. I trust the examples supplied in Chapters 5-7 will be informative, illustrative, and challenging. Chapter 8 raises the question of our next step.

This is in no way the final word on either cell church or Natural Church Development. My first desire is that those of us within the cell church movement will be challenged to take more seriously the work of NCD and learn to integrate cell and NCD principles. My other desire is for those already employing NCD to also consider the benefits of a cell paradigm.

2

A Bird's Eye View of NCD

IT IS LIKE THE PRECIOUS OIL UPON THE HEAD, COMING DOWN UPON THE BEARD, EVEN AARON'S BEARD, COMING DOWN UPON THE EDGE OF HIS ROBES.

IT IS LIKE THE DEW OF HERMON COMING DOWN UPON THE MOUNTAINS OF ZION; FOR THERE THE LORD COMMANDED THE BLESSING—LIFE FOREVER.
PSALM 133:2-3

Chapter 2 ☛ A Bird's Eye View of NCD

Over the years I have done rather extensive premarital counseling. How often I have seen prospective lifetime partners ready to take the most solemn of earthly vows and to begin the process of two becoming one, when in reality they simply have not spent time enough getting to really know one another! They rarely really know what their prospective partner thinks and feels about the vital issues of life. Only recently, I had a couple break off their engagement after four pre-marital sessions. Why? One party discovered too many incompatibilities in the realm of finances, spirituality, and character. They, like so many before them, had pressed for "marriage now, counseling later". Though saddened by their breakup, how much sadder indeed they would have been to have attempted a marriage when they should never have been married in the first place. Both had already experienced that unfortunate result in their past.

On the other hand, I remember a couple I married in the early 90's. Today they have two beautiful children, a solid marriage, and are continuing to discover how to grow closer together. The premarital counseling often progressed at a snail's pace as they faced painful issues in their lives, both individually and together. They discovered how God could make the whole greater than the sum of the individual parts. They discovered how if one could chase a thousand, then two would chase ten thousand (Deuteronomy 32:30).

I am suggesting a marriage between the principles of cell church and Natural Church Development. I am suggesting not only compatibility, but I am suggesting that if a cell church paradigm can chase a thousand, the union of a cell church paradigm with the NCD paradigm can chase ten thousand. The whole will be far greater than the sum of the parts. But, alas, I have observed too little understanding and much misapplication of NCD principles in the cell church world, and general misinformation regarding cells by many non-cell churches already engaged in the NCD process. Allow me to paint two typical, yet real, scenarios.

In the first scenario, a cell church is encouraged to employ the NCD survey as a health assessment tool. The NCD survey, as you will discover, does assess a church's current health. However, the poorly informed "expert" that encouraged the survey went on to comment as to his motivation, "People tend to be much more receptive to bad news when it comes from an objective outsider who has nothing to gain than from an insider who might be perceived as having too much to gain." The purpose of the survey was to convey "bad news", i.e. the minimum factor, to the powers that be in the hope that a sense of urgency could be generated and change effected. Contrast this "desire to generate a sense of urgency" with an excerpt from a typical Coaching letter sent to a church who has completed the survey:

> The NCD Survey is normed for churches in the USA so that 50 is the median score or "average." Seventy percent of churches taking the survey will score in the range between 35 and 65. The balance of churches taking the survey show fifteen percent scoring above 65 and fifteen percent scoring below 35.
> Please remember…every church has a minimum factor! Do not react emotionally to the results, but think them through carefully and pray that the Lord will help you use this information in a positive way to improve your church and impact your community. Set the tone with your staff and church leaders by emphasizing the opportunity to focus your energy in a way that you can become all that God intends for His church.

There is a great gulf between using a survey to identify minimum factors which every church has, and using a survey to generate a sense of urgency based upon bad news. While the "expert" was the bearer of bad news, the letter came as an encouragement. As Christian Schwartz (NCD, 108) comments:

> There is no church without a "minimum factor." The term does not necessarily mean that a church is "bad" in a certain area–we have even identified churches whose minimum factor area is a model for other churches! It simply means that the seven other areas are better developed than the minimum factor. It also means that concentrating on that low point will bring lasting progress in that congregation's development.

The second scenario, also real, is also, I am afraid, too typical. A certain pastor was given the book *Natural Church Development*. He devoured it. He passed on to his staff members not the book, but the booklet, *ABC's of Natural Church Development*. Although this economical booklet can be used to communicate the principles to a larger number of people in the church

Chapter 2 ☛ A Bird's Eye View of NCD

family, armed with this general and minimal understanding, his staff was then requested to rank the highest and lowest factor. Seeing that they all ranked the minimum and maximum factors alike, almost immediately the leadership of the church felt an urgency to change.

Such misuse by a pastor may very well become, in the long term, detrimental for the church. In all likelihood, their assessment is in error, leading them to urgently attempt to "fix" the wrong problem. Why does such intuition, even on the part of pastors and staff, often fail? Listen again to Schwartz's comments, taken from the very book the pastor in question read, but failed to comprehend (NCD, 108):

> Over the past years, I have noticed that when people try to identify their church's minimum factors by intuition alone, they are often off the mark. In fact, it is not unusual for them to think that the area of their greatest strength is their minimum factor!
>
> How can this happen? Usually these churches have extremely high quality standards in this area. They also have a developed awareness of all potential problems, and, therefore, a keen eye for possible improvements. Other areas of church life that are not so important to them, however, they hardly seem to notice. To reliably identify a church's minimum factors–instead of going on assumptions–I recommend that every church obtain a church profile based on a scientifically sound analysis.

Birds have a unique advantage over man. Birds are able to soar in the heavens and see the whole, view the overall. Then they can swoop down to the details below. We too often are stuck in the mire of the details, rarely seeing the whole picture from a distance. Toward this end is the present chapter directed.

So that we are enabled to see the whole before attempting to apply the pieces to our cell churches, the remainder of this chapter will attempt to overview the history of the NCD research and basic NCD concepts. This should by no means be construed as in any way exhaustive and the reader is encouraged to obtain original documentation for more extensive study and understanding.

WHAT IS NATURAL CHURCH DEVELOPMENT?

"Natural (or biotic) church development is an attempt to study nature, and thus God's creation, to discover principles that are applicable far beyond the realm of biology. This appeal to the biological world, the 'largest and most successful organizational system we know,' involves the use of *analogy* as a method of perception. This analogy is not concentrated on the external appearances; rather it attempts to 'press on to the underlying basic principles'." (Paradigm, 233)

Frederic Vester writes: "Even more productive than the study of biological structures and functions is what we can learn from the organization of biological processes, from the specific dynamics of their development and decomposition, their growth, their communication, and their self-regulation." (Paradigm, 233).

When we are told by Jesus to observe how the lilies of the field grow, not to concentrate on the lilies themselves but on their growth mechanisms, we are informed that we are to do so in order that we might come to understand the principles of the Kingdom of God. This approach describes the procedure employed by Natural Church Development.

The quest of Natural Church Development is the discovery and application of growth automatisms in the work of the church, the Body of Christ.

A Different Way of Thinking About Growth

Natural Church Development (NCD) is a **paradigm** – a way of thinking about church growth. Growth should be about quality (health) and not just quantity (numbers). In fact, NCD suggests that quality should take priority over quantity in church growth thinking.

At the heart of the paradigm is the scriptural picture of the church as a living organism, not just an organization (albeit a spiritual one). Looking at the church organically gives us a different perspective on what growth means. The growth of organisms focuses on their health, their capacity to reproduce, and how the individual body parts interact. They are grown, not built. They are nurtured, not assembled.

The NCD paradigm suggests that if church growth is about growing an organism, the <u>health</u> (quality) of the organism is going to have a direct impact on its <u>size</u> (quantity). If a church can become increasingly healthy over time, it is more likely and better able to reproduce disciples, ministries and eventually itself. The NCD paradigm helps one think about growing the church as a healthy living organism.

A Long-Term Strategic Process

Natural Church Development is also a long-term strategic **process** for progressively improving a church's health. It is a process of continual improvement, not a program that, if implemented to the letter, guarantees "a healthy church." It requires a long-term commitment that is intentional and consistent.

Natural Church Development is a **strategy**. While principles merely describe universally valid individual insights, a strategy integrates these principles together and forges a systematic overall concept. The result is a rough framework from within which programs can be derived. The eight quality characteristics of growing churches described later on in this chapter are in fact principles abstracted from the study of thousands of churches.

At the heart of the process is a sophisticated diagnostic tool, the NCD survey, which complies with international statistical standards for validity and reliability. Annual surveys provide an accurate up-to-date "snapshot" of the health of the church on an ongoing basis. They are based on an assessment by key people within the life of the church. Each survey enables the church leadership to assess improvement in the church's health over the previous year and to focus on the specific area needing the greatest attention during the coming year.

The strategy of Natural Church Development is built upon three building blocks. The eight quality characteristics together form the first building block. The six biotic principles unite to create the second building block. The third building block is the minimum strategy. (Paradigm, 240)

However, before turning our attention to the basic building blocks of NCD, allow me to briefly review with you its origins and research.

ORIGINS AND CONTINUING RESEARCH

Worldwide Research

The Institute for Natural Church Development International, based in Germany under the leadership of Christian Schwarz, undertook a worldwide research project in the early 1990s. The original study from 1994 through 1996 is the most thorough study to date of the factors leading to church growth. One thousand churches in thirty-two (32) countries were surveyed to determine if there were principles producing healthy church growth independent of denomination or theology, country or culture, leadership style, size, or ministry model. The responses, 4.2 million, were then tabulated. The key question the Institute sought to answer was, "**What church growth principles are true, regardless of culture and theological persuasion?**"

The research revealed a framework of eight quality characteristics that were operating in healthy, growing churches. All were present and none could be missing. They were:

- Empowering Leadership
- Gift-oriented Ministry
- Passionate Spirituality
- Functional Structures
- Inspiring Worship
- Holistic Small Groups
- Need-Oriented Evangelism
- Loving Relationships

The result of the study was that growing churches clearly scored above the qualitative median in each of the eight categories, and declining churches were similarly below the median. The research further revealed that there was no one single factor which led to growth in churches; it was the interplay of all eight elements. What was considered the most spectacular discovery of the survey was the fact that there was one rule for which they did not find a single exception among the 1000 churches surveyed. Namely, every church in which a quality index of 65 or more was reached for each of the eight quality characteristics was a growing church. The "65 hypothesis" simply states that whenever all eight values climb to 65, the statistical probability that the church is growing is 99.4 percent.

Research has continued into the present. By 2002 the Institute had expanded its research into 50 countries, profiled 12,000 churches, and tabulated over 45 million responses.

BUILDING BLOCK #1: EIGHT QUALITY CHARACTERISTICS

Natural Church Development "does not approach the question of church growth from the perspective of its quantitative effects, but (deliberately) from the perspective of the underlying spiritual and strategic causes." (Paradigm, 241) Lest NCD be accused of playing quality off against quantity, it must be noted that there is an implicit assumption that real quality, as against supposed quality, generally does have an effect on quantity. After all, the Bible is clear, a good tree will produce good fruit (Matthew 7:17).

"To some extent, each quality characteristic contains the heart of all other elements; conversely, none of the elements can be put into practice effectively if we do not also work on the other areas." (Paradigm, 242)

I am indebted to Robert Logan (Releasing, 1.8-1.10) for the following definitions of the eight quality characteristics displayed by growing churches throughout the world.

Empowering Leadership

Effective leadership begins with an intimate relationship with God, resulting in Christ-like character and a clear sense of God's calling for leaders' lives. As this base of spiritual maturity increases, effective pastors and leaders multiply, guide, empower and equip disciples to realize their full potential in Christ and work together to accomplish God's vision.

Gift-Oriented Ministry

The Holy Spirit sovereignly gives to every Christian spiritual gift(s) for the building of God's kingdom. Church leaders have the responsibility to help believers discover, develop and exercise their gifts in appropriate ministries so that the Body of Christ "grows and builds itself up in love."

Passionate Spirituality

Effective ministry flows out of a passionate spirituality. Spiritual intimacy leads to a strong conviction that God will act in powerful ways. A godly vision can only be accomplished through an optimistic faith that views obstacles as opportunities and turns defeats into victories.

Functional Structures

The Church is the living Body of Christ. Like all healthy organisms, it requires numerous systems that work together to fulfill its intended purpose. Each must be evaluated regularly to determine if it is still the best way to accomplish the intended purpose.

Inspiring Worship

Inspiring Worship is a personal and corporate encounter with the living God. Both personal and corporate worship must be infused with the presence of God resulting in times of joyous exultation and times of quiet reverence. Inspiring worship is not driven by a particular style or ministry focus group – but rather the shared experience of God's awesome presence.

Holistic Small Groups

Holistic small groups are disciple-making communities which endeavor to reach the unchurched, meet individual needs, develop each person according to their God-given gifts and raise leaders to sustain the growth of the church. Like healthy body cells, holistic small groups are designed to grow and multiply.

Need-Oriented Evangelism

Need-oriented evangelism intentionally cultivates relationships with pre-Christian people so they can become fully-devoted followers of Jesus Christ who are actively participating within the life of the church and community. Using appropriate ministries and authentic relationships, believers can guide others into the family of God.

Loving **Relationships**

Loving relationships are the heart of a healthy, growing church. Jesus said people will know we are His disciples by our love. Practical demonstration of love builds authentic Christian community and brings others into God's kingdom.

BUILDING BLOCK #2: SIX BIOTIC PRINCIPLES

In January 2000, NCD released *The Challenge of Implementing the Biotic Principles*. The document, prepared by Direction Ministry Resources, was designed to be a guide for use with the the *Minimum Factor Manual*. Unless otherwise noted, I am indebted to *The Challenge of Implementing the Biotic Principles* for the understanding, the concepts and the definitions which follow.

What are the Biotic Principles?

Christian Schwarz defines the biotics as principles of God which work in the biological world. The research shows that these produce sustainable, healthy growth when operating in churches. The name "biotic" is from 'bios' meaning life – they are principles for *releasing life within the church*.

The biotic principles encourage leadership to look at the whole church and its environment and not just "the fruit" as an indicator of health. They focus on the way a church "does church".

Whereas the quality characteristics indicate **what** needs to be addressed, the biotic principles are concerned with **how** a church addresses the quality characteristics *through its fabric of operation*. As Schwarz clearly notes:

> Whereas the eight quality characteristics are concerned with the content, that is, with the question "What?", the biotic principles are concerned with the question "How?" To put it in a nutshell: the more we apply the biotic principles in each of the eight areas mentioned, the greater the growth potential of a church will be.

> The six biotic principles are meant to be rules that can help us in every issue to make decisions. This principle-oriented approach sets natural church development apart from a legalistic *casuistry* ("Follow exactly this method and your church will grow!") on the one hand and mere pragmatism (The end justifies the means!") on the other. Rather, each decision should be made in such a way that it is in harmony with God's principles of growth. (Paradigm, 243-244)

These six principles have been observed in growing churches. Schwarz' contribution has been to give them a name and integrate them in a methodically structured overall strategy. (Paradigm, 244)

A Process for Lasting Change

Natural Church Development is a process based on a new paradigm. The greatest danger with NCD is to implement change with new ideas, focus and enthusiasm but use old methods of thinking and practice.

The biotic principles are integral to the process of releasing the growth automatisms in the church and therefore bringing permanent gains in health, both in quality and quantity. They gradually remove processes which block *automatic growth* and they introduce initiatives which promote *automatic growth*.

Connecting Quality Characteristics and Biotic Principles

The quality characteristics are indicators of health (when measured) and as such provide the **framework** for addressing the issues of health. What distinguishes NCD as both an assessment tool and as a paradigm is its focus on the health of the church through the application of *values* to those eight quality characteristics. This is seen in the adjectives:

- *Empowering* Leadership
- *Gift-oriented* Ministry
- *Passionate* Spirituality
- *Functional* Structures
- *Inspiring* Worship
- *Holistic* Small Groups
- *Need-Oriented* Evangelism
- *Loving* Relationships

Chapter 2 ☞ A Bird's Eye View of NCD

The health paradigm is found not in the nouns, but in the adjectives. For example, the focus to pursue is not leadership, but *empowering* leadership. The adjectives serve as value statements in that NCD will only be effective as a process when church leadership owns them in head, heart and soul.

The challenge before a church embracing NCD is to recognize that it cannot approach the quality characteristics without addressing them as value statements. What faces a church embracing NCD is how to identify, challenge and where necessary change its own values to come in line with the quality characteristic adjectives and to define the adjectives in ways meaningful to that church from a values perspective.

I am not suggesting here that all churches must hold these quality characteristics as core values (See my book, *Preparing the 21st Century Church*). However, I do suggest they should at least be held as secondary values.

The biotic principles thus help you introduce biotic processes which incorporate those values into the fabric of operation of the cell church, thus improving its health. The overall effect is fourfold:

- They move the church away from trying to solve issues by going in search of a program, even a cell program, and instead focus leadership decision making on the more fundamental issues of how the church is actually operating.

- They provide an additional grid for thinking through practical responses.

- They provide a checking mechanism which reinforces the application of each principle.

- They help keep attention on the minimum factor's adjective.

This is a difficult process to embrace, both intellectually and practically. The rewards are great for those prepared to wrestle with the issues. On the other hand, not to do so can make the entire NCD process next to meaningless. Chapters 5, 6, and 7 look at common issues facing cell churches today and illustrate how to begin the process of employing the biotic principles. Where this is applied, ultimately the church operates biotically, the potential is released and growth takes place "all by itself". To avoid the biotic principles and focus only on the quality characteristics is to miss the essence of Natural Church Development.

Applying Biotic Principles

The biotic principles are variations of one single principle: "How can we create an environment that will allow God's growth automatisms – with which He Himself builds the church – ever increasing influence?" Recognizing the interrelated nature of the biotics, all the biotic principles are addressed at once in the context of putting together an action plan.

The NCD approach toward applying the biotic principles to the church is four-fold:

1. Help the church leadership to truly understand each of the biotic principles through individual or group learning sessions.

2. Brainstorm possible initiatives to address the minimum factor using each of the biotic principles in turn without (at this point) reaching definitive courses of action.

3. Examine each of the potential initiatives in light of all six biotic principles, thereby discerning the overlapping nature of the biotic principles.

4. Implement those initiatives which satisfy all six biotic principles.

Biotic Principle #1: Interdependence

Definition

The decision you make in one area of church life will impact, for good or ill, other areas of church life. "We should understand the church as a complex organism in which all parts are linked with all others. The way the different parts are integrated into the whole is more important than the parts themselves. It is therefore important to gain an ever deepening understanding of the nature of this network, rather than just considering isolated activities or an individual segment of church development." (Paradigm, 244)

Statement about Connection

Change to one area of ministry will impact other areas. Action on the biotic principle means learning to monitor and ultimately preempt such impacts. What looks like a good idea on its own for improving the health of the church may have consequences the opposite of what was intended.

Statement about Integration

Interdependence looks at how ministries can move together rather than just focusing on the "parts" doing their own thing and moving independently of one another.

Statement about Proactivity

This is a hard biotic principle to address if church leadership is constantly in reactive or crises mode. There will be little change until the church leadership is prepared to consider long term implications of its decisions. Inherent in this principle is the need for planning. Interdependence is best analyzed in the context of planning, rather than allowing all who come with ministry initiatives to "go and do what is right in their own eyes".

Key Question

Are the long term effects that this measure, step or decision has on other areas of the church organism beneficial for the healthy development of the church or not? (The purpose of the key question is to bring each biotic principle to bear on every step of decision making by the church leadership. Eventually the fabric of operation of the church becomes biotic because decisions are made biotically.)

Biotic Principle #2: Multiplication

Definition

"Behind this principle lies a recognition that unlimited increase in size (permanent addition) is not biotic. At some point, all growth has its natural limits. But in a network system, permanent multiplication is possible and desirable. A plant does not permanently increase in size; instead, it produces new plants, which themselves produce new plants. It is our task to create a structure that enables the work not only to be extended, but to be multiplied." (Paradigm, 244-245)

Statement about Multiplication
Life both begins and grows through a process of multiplication rather than addition. Living organisms are formed by the multiplication of cells. Individual cells die and for the organism to continue living and growing, these cells must multiply.

Statement about Fruitfulness
The biotic processes of nature show multiplication is the process of continuing the life cycle through reproduction. Fruitfulness is measured as growth through reproduction.

Statement about Leadership Focus
The focus of leadership must move to equipping for reproduction. The question is no longer, "Who can I get to do a job I have?" but "How can I reproduce myself in others so that they know their primary role is to reproduce themselves in others...and so on."

Statement about Every Level of Church Life
Reproduction becomes part of every job description in the church. The focus is on people, ministries and churches reproducing themselves. One can begin to see how the biotic element contained in the principle of multiplication starts to impact the value of empowering in a practical way as it relates to the leadership characteristic. This then releases the "all by itself" growth principle which is the overriding concern with all the biotic material.

Key Question
Does this measure, step or decision contain multiplication [reproduction] dynamics or is it merely about addition?

Biotic Principle #3: Energy Transformation

Definition
Focus all energy in the church on generating growth in the church's health by forcing all energies (including hostile) to be turned in the right direction through minute steering strategies. "This principle is concerned with harnessing and controlling the contrary forces existent in the environment. Instead of destroying the forces of nature by using counter force ('boxer mentality'), the principle of energy transformation utilizes them by using leverage." (Paradigm, 245)

Statement about Energy Identification
Where is the energy being generated in the church, both negatively and positively, and what about? Being too busy or in crises mode may mean missing the negative and positive forces that are emerging.

Statement about Energy Conservation and Re-direction
The response to any energy forces identified is to think growth. How can this energy, whether expressed negatively or positively, be harnessed for the good of the whole body? How can your energy and their energy be re-directed from competition to cooperation? What course of action will harness the energy here to bring health to the church?

Statement about Priorities and Motivation
To conserve energy, leaders must learn to make wise decisions about what is worth "the good fight". Leaders should be alert to issues which demotivate, disempower and de-energize the Body.

Key Question
Is this measure, step or decision utilizing the energy relationships of the church environment, or trying to fight them?

Biotic Principle #4: Multi-usage

Definition
Energy spent can be re-invested to make this ministry, program or process increasingly self-sustaining. The setting up of processes whereby energy, once invested, is put to many uses to reinforce and build the ministry in which it is invested.

Statement about Flexibility & Resource Usage
People will undoubtedly function best within their giftings, but for the sake of the Body adaptation is vital. The tendency is for people to focus on a particular selection of gifts. It is more a reflection of the spirit of the age that churches are producing a bunch of specialists not a group of well-rounded generalists who have specialist skills in particular areas. Multi-usage involves developing generic process which can be duplicated across the church where appropriate. The biotic focus here is on the flexibility of parts of the body to move in to support areas of weakness (multi-usage). The danger is generating competition for resources.

Statement about Reinventing the Wheel
This biotic principle has an added dimension of an energy cycle of investment rather than a one way street. The multi-usage comes in terms of the mentality a leader adopts when expending time and energy on something. Rather than just repeating a ministry task, program or process over and over again, a portion of that time should be given to making sure the task, program or process is self-sustaining. The time spent thus has a multiple usage.

Key Question
Do the results of this measure, step or decision show this ministry to be increasingly *self-sustaining*?

Biotic Principle #5: Symbiosis

Definition
The intimate living together of two dissimilar organisms in a mutually beneficial relationship. In short, building win-win relationships.

Statement about Interdependence
This biotic principle is concerned that an initiative is mutually advantageous to all the parties impacted. Will all affected by or participating in this initiative gain from it? While the principle of interdependence cause the leadership to stop and ask what impact this initiative will have on existing ministries, that is, what other boats will get rocked when this one is launched into the bay, the principle of symbiosis comes from the other direction and asks which ministries will benefit from being linked to this ministry. That is, which ministries will bring win-win- relationships? While interdependence is concerned with preventing conflict, symbiosis is concerned with actively promoting cooperation instead of competition.

Statement about Synergy
The outcome is greater than the sum of the parts if people work together closely to achieve certain goals. Note the linkage with energy transformation. There will ultimately be a creation of energy because all the participants see their efforts in cooperation being rewarded.

Statement about Diversity
This principle rejects the robotic model where everything is processed the same way to achieve the same results. Instead, it promotes organic diversity which fits the concept of the church as the Body. whereas energy transformation looks at promoting focused energy together, symbiosis looks at promoting diverse life together. It actively sets about in a practical way to establish working links between ministries that at first glance don't seem to have anything in common.

Statement about Biblical Community
True biblical community is less about achieving tasks than people contributing to the life and growth of others. Only by living together is life

sustained – 'sum' (*with, together*) and 'bios' (*life*). It is the preferred way that fruitfulness occurs rather than the "each person to him or herself" approach. Symbiosis is the principle that deals directly with the individualistic spirit.

Key Question

Does this measure, step or decision contribute to fruitful cooperation of different forms of ministry, or does it promote an ecclesiastical monoculture? Does this promote organic diversity (life together) or robotic uniformity (tasks together)?

Biotic Principle #6: Functionality

Definition

"A healthy organism automatically rejects forms that are not conducive to its health. Nothing in nature is an end in itself, always a means to a higher end. All life in God's creation is characterized by its ability to bear fruit." (Paradigm, 246)

Every detail in God's creation has a specific function...All living things in God's creation are characterized by the ability to bear fruit...where there is no fruit, life is condemned to death...We are able to check on the quality of an organism by examining its fruit....Where no fruit appears, something is wrong.

Statement about Purpose and Outcome

Every ministry, structure, activity and process should have a clear purpose or reason for existence. The leadership should be able to say" "This was established to..." The value of ministry lies not in its existence but in the outcome it achieves. Ministries old and new need to undergo regular assessments to determine if they are achieving the purpose for which they are established.

Statement about Change

Ministries, structures, activities and processes may be achieving the original purpose for which they were established, but are they still relevant to where the church is going now?

Statement about Quality

The overall health of the church is made up of the health of the parts of the Body and their interaction. every part of the Body should be examined and tended to regularly to ensure that it continues to contribute to the life of the whole. No area of the church should escape scrutiny.

Key Question

Is this measure producing fruit for the Kingdom of God, or is it missing its purpose?

BUILDING BLOCK #3: THE MINIMUM STRATEGY

"Whereas the quality characteristics describe the content we need to work on (What should we do?) and the biotic principles tell us about the method (How should we do it?), the third building block, the minimum strategy, examines the right timing (When should we do it?)." (Paradigm, 248)

Natural Church Development is based upon the following assumptions. The church will grow quantitatively until growth is impeded by the least developed quality characteristic, its minimum factor. If the church desires to continue to grow, it must deal with this quality characteristic. If it is successful in developing the quality in this area, then quantitative growth will resume and continue until such time as it is impeded again by the next minimum factor. At this point, the church must turn its attention to the new minimum factor and concentrate on a qualitative improvement in this area. The development of the church is thus a constant interplay between qualitative and quantitative factors. In the church, the best results have been achieved when the church's existing strengths have been employed to tackle the church's weakest points, their minimum factor. (Paradigm, 249-250)

The minimum strategy goes back to the biological discoveries of Justus von Liebig. His "quality characteristics" were the four minerals necessary for the growth of plants. His discovery of their interplay with plant growth enabled biological production to be dramatically increased (Paradigm, 249).

BIPOLAR ECCLESIOLOGY

According to Christian Schwarz (Paradigm, 15), "bipolar ecclesiology is of fundamental importance for anyone who is interested in a theological reflection of church growth". He states categorically (Paradigm, 15), "I am now more convinced than ever that the bipolar approach is essential for a theological understanding of church growth; and it is definitely the theological key for understanding what natural church development is all about." If, as Schwarz himself contends, bipolar ecclesiology is the theological key for unlocking the door into Natural Church Development, then we had best understand how to use the key if we would walk through the door. For those readers among us who might anticipate this section to be a bit theologically dry and impractical, let me be quick to add that the lack of such a bipolar ecclesiology within the cell church movement has led to an imbalance between cells and the corporate congregation. A shift in our theology might just shift the cell church back into balance! I will pick up this theme as it relates to cell edification in chapter 3, and as it relates to the corporate body in chapter 5. For those interested in wrestling further with the issues about to be addressed, I would highly recommend a study of Schwarz' work, *Paradigm Shift in the Church*.

The Dynamic and the Static

"The nature of the church is made up of two elements: a dynamic pole (organism) and a static pole (organization). Both are necessary for church development, and both poles are implied in the New Testament concept of *ekklesia*." (Paradigm, 16)

The Nature of the Dynamic Pole

"The dynamic pole is mainly found in New Testament statements which describe the church in biological, organic terms and therefore emphasize the aspect of 'growth.' The prime example is the way the church is characterized as the 'body of Christ,' and the individual Christians as 'parts of the body'." (Paradigm, 16)

The Nature of the Static Pole

"The static element is found in statements which describe the church in terms of architectural and technical metaphors and consequently emphasize the aspect of 'church building.' The prime example is the way the Apostle Paul characterizes himself as a 'wise architect' who laid the 'foundation' on which others 'build'." (Paradigm, 16)

The Relationship between Organization and Organism

Both approaches to understanding the church are present in the New Testament and are in no way in competition with each other. "There are even a number of passages in which the two aspects are so closely intertwined in a single statement that the resulting picture–judged by standards of linear logic–seems contradictory. Examples are such phrases as 'living (organic metaphor) stones (technical metaphor),' 'growing (organic metaphor) into a temple (technical metaphor),' the description of the Corinthians as 'God's field (organic metaphor) and God's building (technical metaphor),' or 'that the body of Christ (organic metaphor) may be built up (technical metaphor)'." (Paradigm, 16)

This polarity expresses the distinction between the church as an organization and the church as an organism. Organization and organism are in a twofold relationship to one another. "The dynamic pole always creates organization (structures, institutions, rules, or programs). The purpose of this organization is, in its turn, to develop further the dynamic pole. As long as this cycle is intact–in practice, not just in out thinking–there is a highly creative relationship between the two poles." (NCD, 85)

While we can have control over the church as an organization and in a sense "manufacture" it, that is never true of the church as an organism. "In natural church development, all we can do...is subject the elements we can influence to the criterion of functionality in such a way that the elements that are beyond our control may take place." (Paradigm, 21)

The cycle connecting the dynamic and static poles can break down in two ways. It is possible to take the institutional pole and treat it as the whole. The presumption is that where this pole exists, the church is present in its fullness. Schwarz calls this imbalance "monism" (NCD, 86):

Monism treats both poles as one. People who are influenced by this thought pattern are convinced that if only the right pole has the right form (right doctrine, right political persuasion, right church growth program, etc.), then they don't have to worry about the left pole (the dynamic life of the organism called the church).

The cycle can also break down when the dynamic pole is separated from its static counterpart and forms, programs, structures and institutions are considered, at best, spiritually irrelevant, and at worst, downright harmful. Schwarz calls this view "dualism". (NCD, 86)

How can we better understand the somewhat abstract terms of monism and dualism? An illustration from music may help clarify the issues. Christian Schwarz writes:

> To hear music from stereo equipment requires two poles, two loudspeakers. A monistic approach in this context would be like listening to a recording in a reduced "mono" mode, claiming that the music is terrific and fully convinced that the one loudspeaker reflects "the whole".
>
> On the other hand, dualistic thinking would be like insisting that only the left speaker is ever needed, because the right speaker is unnecessary for enjoying the wonderful music, and might even be dangerous. The truth of the matter is that God has given us two ears–another bipolarity in His creation–and thus the way we enjoy music must take this bipolarity into account.
>
> This illustration shows us that the two positions are in one sense quite different: monism treats both poles as one, dualism disconnects the poles. But they have one thing in common, however: they are both incapable of a bipolar view. Monistic thinking in church growth leads easily to technocratic approaches ("Follow this program, and your church will grow"). Dualistic thinking, on the other hand, often produces an anti-institutional spiritualism ("Institutions are spiritually irrelevant"). Both are far removed from the reality God the Creator has placed in humanity; both impede biblical thinking;

Chapter 2 ☛ A Bird's Eye View of NCD

both hinder living faith–and both frustrate efforts to seek church growth and development as well. (NCD, 86-87)

Most Christians think either dualistically or monistically, spiritualistically or technocratically. This lopsided thinking is unfortunately also evident and prevalent within the cell church movement. In the next two chapters, we will examine the results of such thinking in the cell church movement, as we consider how to release stereophonic cell ministry and grow stereophonic cell churches.

3

RELEASING STEREOPHONIC CELL MINISTRY

Now there are varieties of gifts, but the same Spirit. And there are varieties of ministries, and the same Lord. There are varieties of effects, but the same God who works all things in all persons. But to each one is given the manifestation of the Spirit for the common good.   1 Corinthians 12:4-7

Chapter 3 ☛ *Releasing Stereophonic Cell Ministry*

I am old enough to remember the first stereo systems. I grew up playing 45 rpm singles and 33 rpm records. I had one speaker out of which Beethoven's 9th Symphony, as well as his previous eight, would blare forth. To really feel the music, I would have to "pump up the volume". Try as I might to distinguish the parts comprising the whole, I could only listen to the whole. Was I satisfied at the time? Sure. It was not nearly as good as buying tickets for Chicago's Ravinia Theatre where I was able to both watch and listen as Igor Stravinsky, a great conductor from yester-year, turned simple instruments into a symphony, but it was all I had. I could only dream of better days to come.

I remember my first job–working hard to save so I could purchase that stereo system. Dual speakers. How novel! How did they get, not just the same music coming out of both speakers, but different music? It was a miracle!Beethoven sounded so, well, different! The 9th Symphony was richer, fuller, like the composer meant it to be. Having tasted of stereo, I never wanted to return to mono listening. Even as I write, the background is filled with the strains of David Ruis' *Let the Winds Blow*–in stereo!

I am also old enough to remember early attempts to bring edification to God's people, in mono.

VIEWING EDIFICATION THROUGH BIPOLAR LENSES

Much is written about edification in cell literature today. There seems to be an almost unspoken assumption that we both know what edification is and are engaged in its practice. Yet, is that really the truth?

Scott Boren, in his well written book, *Making Cell Groups Work*, writes of the ministry of edification (58):

> Basic Christian community is an experience of Christ in the midst of a group of people who know one another, love one another, and support one another. It is the knowledge that Jesus has come to life by His Spirit moving through every member of the body.
> The ministry of edification is stated in the Great Commandment: "Love the Lord your God with all your heart

and with all your soul and with all your mind. This is the first and greatest commandment. And the second is like it: Love your neighbor as yourself" (Matthew 22:37-39)....The ministry of edification and expansion is the call of every church. It is also the call of every believer. The same call should form the foundation for every cell group.

Joel Comiskey (How, 13) defines a small group or cell as a "group of people (4-5), who meet regularly for the purpose of spiritual edification and evangelistic outreach (with the goal of multiplication), who are committed to participate in the functions of the local church."

For years on the American small group scene, the emphasis has been on edification, to the detriment of leadership development, evangelism and multiplication. Far too frequently American small groups have been "Bless Me Clubs", "Christian Hot Tubs", and for "Us Four and No More". I applaud and wholeheartedly agree with the present challenge to evangelize and multiply. I threw my own hat into the ring with my first book, *Preparing the 21st Century Church*.

Yet, I would challenge the notion that we both understand and practice the ministry of edification. I believe we have approached edification either dualistically or monistically, spiritualistically or technocratically, rather than through bipolar lenses. This has led to weakened and/or ineffective edification in our cells week to week and ultimately weak or sickly holistic small groups. Whether you are seeking to have healthy cells or great holistic small groups, bipolar thinking can help maintain our sense of balance. Allow me to illustrate our monistic and dualistic approach, and then suggest a bipolar approach releasing stereophonic cell ministry. If we could somehow transform our current edification paradigm into a bipolar paradigm, our holistic small groups would be greatly strengthened and the church built up in the faith.

Monism – Technocratic Paradigm

The institutionalistic misunderstanding stems from the identification of the church as an organization and the church as an organism with one another. Instead of evaluating the organizational nature of the church from a

Chapter 3 — Releasing Stereophonic Cell Ministry

functional point of view, the organization is assumed to have an almost magical quality about it. In other words, there is the implicit assumption that whenever certain institutions, structures, or forms are present, the church of Jesus is guaranteed. This misconception takes a variety of forms and characteristics.

One such characteristic is objectivism. "Objectivism arises out of an understandable human drive for security. People are not content with the *certitudo* of faith; rather, they seek the *securitas* which always tries to reassure itself with guarantees." (Paradigm, 25) Instead of viewing the forms of cell as being useful to stimulate the organic side of the church, i.e., the work of the Holy Spirit in edification, those well meaning cell leaders blindsided here want the presence of Christ to be guaranteed. The cell as an organism becomes unnecessary. Consequently, cell leaders refuse to change their cell "liturgy" (welcome, worship, word, works) even in the face of apparent needs for ministry at the "wrong" time, because people will be edified as they maintain the "correct" cell format (structure).

Let's examine another characteristic of the technocratic paradigm–formalism. What! cells lapse into formalism! How can such a thing be? Consider the training of cell leaders. We can see here a rationalistic variety of formalism. For too long, the training of cell leaders has placed the emphasis almost exclusively on the rational standards of knowledge. Although there have been recent attempts at revamping cell training to incorporate psychomotor and affective training alongside the cognitive instruction, most traditional training focuses on the cognitive development of the students. Scott Boren notes (Making, 299):

> Some churches have taken the equipping journey process and created a class like Christianity 101, Discipleship 201, Ministry 301, and Leadership 401. While the intent and the content of these classes is usually excellent, church leaders often fall into the trap of parading people through the classes. They expect the graduates to mature but they only gain more head knowledge about God. They expect new leaders from the 401 class, but the graduates do not seem ready.

Joel Comiskey's challenge toward bipolarity (not his choice of words) in learning to lead cells is refreshing, especially as a word of warning in a book whose primary purpose is to serve as a how-to manual. Joel warns his readers (How, 25):

> This book emphasizes the importance of small group techniques. Yet, in this chapter, I've warned you not to follow techniques too closely. I've said, "Let the Spirit guide you." "Be open to analyze each situation with Spirit anointed common sense." Sound like a contradiction? Not really. Plans, techniques and diligent preparation for the small group meeting are exceedingly important **[static pole]**. Just don't allow them to control you **[technocratic-formalism]**. That's the Spirit's job. As you spend time in His presence, you'll make better plans **[dynamic pole stimulating static pole]**, know how to handle each situation, and meet the needs of those present. [Bracketed bold text is this author's addition.]

One last example should suffice here. To use Jesus' example of the farmer again, the technocratic paradigm would place all the weight and responsibility squarely on the farmer's shoulders. Everything is up to the farmer. Or, in our application, the weight of edification is up to the cell leader or member. If they do it just right, saying the right words when praying in Jesus Name, they will be assured that edification will take place. Unfortunately that is not a balanced approach.

Dualism – Spiritualistic Paradigm

The mistake of institutionalism is to identify as one organization and organism. The mistake of spiritualism is to separate the two poles.

A characteristic of the spiritualistic paradigm is subjectivism. The subjectivists make their religious experience the standard by which everything is judged. What drives the spiritualistic paradigm? It is the desire for unconditional freedom and spontaneity. All is left up to the Spirit. He inspires and does His work when and how He wills.

A second characteristic, dualism, explains why spiritualists have a hard time understanding and accepting the strategical implications of church development. They see no meaning in anything like church analysis.

Planning, strategy, and principles all carry negative emotions. If it is all of the Spirit, then man can contribute nothing.

How does this understanding affect our cell life? Cell leaders feel constrained by any cell liturgy. Far from feeling "I must lead cell just this way in order for the presence of Christ to be manifest", cell leaders in this ditch resist any liturgy at all. "Why must I use the pattern of Welcome, Worship, Word, Works? Why can I not just follow the leading of the Spirit each week?" Using the pastor's message as the topic of discussion is too limiting. "I must have the freedom and spontaneity to lead as I feel the Holy Spirit directing." They see little or no use in filling out forms, which is why their weekly cell reports are frequently late and often missing. Cell multiplication will happen according to the move of the Spirit, not on any regular schedule. There is no use in planning cell, multiplication, or in any way engaging in strategy planning with their coach. They claim they are just not "wired" that way.

Edification is incorrectly viewed as simply a sovereign work of God. One must merely look to the Spirit's move and go with the flow. Man has no part but to receive, and no responsibility after the Spirit does His work. The religious experience of the one edified is the measure by which they judge how well edification has taken place. Is it any wonder that the same people with the same problems need "edification", a "fresh touch of the Spirit," every week in cell? To question their activity and/or thinking leaves their critic open to the charge of being legalistic or unspiritual.

Bipolar Approach

What is a bipolar approach to edification? What will it entail? What will it look like? These are the questions the remainder of this chapter will address. For now, let us simply say that adopting a bipolar approach to edification will mean embracing a static pole encompassing what is humanly possible and a dynamic pole encompassing what only God can do.

1 Corinthians 3:6 is a key verse. "I planted, Apollos watered, but God gives the increase." Paul and Apollos could plant, water, and even harvest. Their diligence in planting and watering did have an influence on the harvest to come. However, what they could not do was cause the growth to occur. Applied to edification, there is that which man can do, and should do, and even must do. Our actions will, in the final analysis, affect the process of edi-

fication. However, only God can actually perform the activity of edification. What can we do? We can ensure that the static (right) pole of cell life is in harmony with God's principles. Doing so will not in any way guarantee the dynamics of the left pole, but it will stimulate the organic pole. Doing so will posture us before God and help create an environment in which the Spirit is free to engage in His work. This then becomes our approach to cell edification and releasing stereophonic cell ministry.

DYNAMIC PARTNERSHIP - JESUS AND ME

When we begin to examine the dynamic partnership between Jesus and the believer in the realm of edification, we find some exhortations in the Scriptures that apply to the static pole, our responsibility, and some exhortations that apply to the dynamic pole, God's responsibility. Examine closely the chart on the following page.

Edification is the guiding principle of cell life. There is one rule which applies to everything which happens within the Basic Christian Community, the cell. Everything must serve to build up the community (1 Corinthians 14:12, 17, 26; Romans 14:19; 15:2; 1 Thessalonians 5:11; Ephesians 4:29). Thus the gifts of grace and offices are judged according to what they contribute to the building up of the community (1 Corinthians 14:3-5; Ephesians 4:29), not according to mere spiritual experience.

Paul scolds the Corinthians: "Knowledge puffs up, but love builds up" (1 Corinthians 18:1). In 1 Corinthians 10:23 Paul corrects the Corinthian slogan, *panta exestin*, "All things are lawful", by urging people to ask themselves whether their actions are conducive to building up the community.

Believers are to be rooted and grounded in Christ (Colossians 2:7). The Christian community is built up together in the co-operation of all the participants (1 Corinthians 3:10-14), and in the unity with apostles and prophets (Ephesians 2:20), to become the one holy community of the Lord.

Edification thus becomes the Head, Christ, beginning to minister to His body through other body members — Christ ministers to me through other body members; Christ ministers through me to other body members.

Chapter 3 ☞ *Releasing Stereophonic Cell Ministry*

God's Activity	Man's Activity
Ephesians 2:22 ...in whom you also are **being built together** into a dwelling of God in the Spirit. **Ephesians 4:11-12** And **He gave some**...for the equipping of the saints for the work of service, **to the building up** of the body of Christ; **Colossians 2:7** ...having been firmly rooted and now **being built up** in Him and established in your faith, just as you were instructed, and overflowing with gratitude. **1 Peter 2:5** You also, as living stones, **are being built up** as a spiritual house for a holy priesthood, to offer up spiritual sacrifices acceptable to God through Jesus Christ.	**Romans 14:19** So then let us pursue the things which make for peace and the **building up** of one another. **Romans 15:2** Let each of us please his neighbor for his good, to his **edification.** **1 Corinthians 14:12** So also you, since you are zealous of spiritual gifts, seek to abound for the **edification** of the church. **Ephesians 4:29** Let no unwholesome word proceed from your mouth, but only such a word as is good for **edification** according to the need of the moment, that it may give grace to those who hear. **1 Thessalonians 5:11** Therefore encourage one another, and **build up** one another, just as you also are doing. **Jude 1:20** But you, beloved, **building** yourselves **up** on your most holy faith; praying in the Holy Spirit;

Jesus - The Master Edifier

When considering this divine partnership, we must admit that Jesus alone is the master edifier. We are on slippery ice and dangerous ground when we lose sight of this reality and our cells become spiritual-problem-solving-cells rather than cells being edified by Christ. A spiritual-problem-solving-cell taps the pooled ability, wisdom and resources of the cell. A cell being edified by Christ taps the spiritual power, wisdom and resources of God. Our cells can degenerate into spiritual-problem-solving cells in at least three ways.

This can happen if the cell sees itself as the source of edification, rather than as a conduit for Christ's edification process. It can occur when an individual brings a need to the cell instead of first bringing it to the foot of the cross. It can take place when a leader or member is perceived (in their own mind, the mind of the cell or the mind of any other member) as the official "edifier" who has the answer or formula to all the problems and needs.

For His part, Jesus decides how He will edify, where the edification will take place, who He will use, and when He will edify His people.

There are many ways Jesus brings about edification to His people. Sometimes He moves in a sovereign direct way, bypassing human agency and directly touching the individual, or speaking to their heart, or providing revelation to their mind and/or spirit, or a combination of the above. Even then we must not limit how He may in a direct way build up His church. At other times, and I believe most of the time in cells, He will employ a human agent. We become His mouth, speaking that which brings upbuilding through prophecy, revelation, or wisdom. We become His hands, hands of compassion and healing. At such times our obedient activity provides an atmosphere which releases His Spirit and stimulates His activity of edification.

Where might the edification take place? I have seen deliverance occur on bedroom floors. I have seen healing happen at kitchen tables. Deep wounds from the past have been revealed by revelation and healed while seated on living room chairs. The touch of God through His people has been evidenced on deck chairs on a back porch and on sidewalks out front. There is no "special place" where edification has to take place. He is free to edify anywhere, anyhow.

Who will He use as His instruments of upbuilding? God is no respecter of persons. He uses the young and the old. His instruments of grace are male and female alike. We will speak more of this when we consider the means of edification.

When will He bring edification to cell members? The most common response to this question is, "During the Word portion of the cell meeting." While this may be true in the general sense, be careful about a formalistic approach that misses His moving at other times.

Worship was designed as a dialogue, not a monologue. As the cell

Chapter 3 ☞ Releasing Stereophonic Cell Ministry

responds to the revelation of the Lord with worship, we should expect the Lord to speak back! Prophecy, tongues, interpretation, revelation, all these and more may provide evidences of His response.

But what about the Welcome? I recall a powerful cell that never went past the Welcome question. A first time visitor in crisis poured forth his heart in response to the welcome question. God touched Him powerfully over the next hour, preparing him to face Monday morning. On another occasion the time of welcome had passed and in the quiet of what could have been an awkward silence, a man's voice blurted out, "I don't have what you all have. Can I get that tonight?" In short order Eugene and his wife Sheryl both made commitments to Christ. Was the cell edified? Yes! Did it happen at the "right" time? You bet it did. It happened right on the Lord's schedule.

Even though we may be expecting God to move to encourage and build up His church as we share around the Word, He often still surprises us in how He does it. Allow me to illustrate by elaborating on the story just noted above. I remember well that cell meeting in the living room of a fairly small trailer in the dead of winter in Grand Forks, North Dakota. The ice breaker had done its job. We had connected with one another and felt at ease. The previous Sunday's sermon text was Revelation 4:1. It dealt with "the door". The leading question was simple and straightforward. "Share briefly how you entered the door of salvation through Jesus." Two or three cell members shared for what all together was not more than 10-12 minutes. There followed one of those "awkward silences" we all dread so much. It was broken by the "visitor's" voice. "I don't have that in my life. Can I get that tonight?" The group was stunned. Having ascertained the "visitor" meant to do business right there on the spot, I knelt down beside him, prayed a short prayer out loud and turned it over to him. As he prayed, confessed and repented, his wife beside him began to weep. When he was done, he looked different. Before anyone else could say or do anything, his wife blurted out that God had shown her while he prayed that she was not really a Christian after all and needed to receive Christ too. She then also prayed and settled the issue. Was the cell edified by the birth of these two new believers? You bet it was! The remainder of the evening was totally transformed. God altered the "cell agenda". The cell received tremendous edification that night simply as God revealed Himself for who He is — Lord and Savior.

Sometimes edification happens when you think you're done and ready to leave. I recall another cell meeting. It had not been a very eventful cell time. The worship had been good, but not exceptional. The sharing had been honest and open. We knew God had been there and we felt built up even though there had not been any personal ministry time. We were standing in a circle holding hands, preparing to close, when it happened. One of the ladies began to tremble, then collapsed on the floor. As the cell gathered around her and began to pray, demonic manifestations began. For the next hour I watched as God used nearly everyone in the cell to minister to their sister. Words of knowledge, prophecy, wisdom, discerning of spirits, even tongues were manifested in a way to deliver and build up. When it was over, she was exhausted, but free! The cell broke into a time of joyful fellowship. She, though, went to sleep on the host's couch. The host let her spend the night while her husband left to take care of the children at home. The next day, Saturday, both families gathered together for an early morning breakfast.

Jesus is the Master edifier. As we have noted, this is a divine partnership with those ministering. However, as those *receiving* ministry, do we have a part in this process? Yes! We must submit ourself, along with our hurt, need or problem to Christ. We must submit to Christ's Body because Christ will edify through His Body. We must be willing to receive the Word that the Lord gives to His Body regarding the issue at hand, its root causes, when it should be dealt with, and how it is to be dealt with.

The Model for Edification

Is there a "correct" model for edification? If by that question we mean, "Is there a model of edification that will guarantee the moving of God's Spirit?" then the answer is, "No." An institutional mindset would like to reduce edification to such cause and effect. However, if by that question we are asking, "Is there a model that may provide a favorable atmosphere for the release of God's edifying Spirit as opposed to other models which may create hindrances to His moving?", then the answer is, "Yes!" Consider with me what I believe to be a positive model for edification, and then contrast that with four faulty and negative models I have also observed being practiced.

A Positive Example - The Pastoral Model

The model I suggest we embrace is the pastoral, shepherd model of the Lord Jesus (John 10:11; Matthew 9:35-39). God cares for His sheep, and

Chapter 3 — Releasing Stereophonic Cell Ministry

He has come to minister to those who are lost, imprisoned, discouraged and wounded. In Ezekiel 34, God leveled a series of indictments against the shepherds of Israel. They had been feeding themselves and neglecting God's flock (verse 2). The Lord said, "You have not strengthened the weak or healed the sick or bound up the injured. You have not brought back the strays or searched for the lost. You have ruled them harshly and brutally. So they were scattered because there was no shepherd...." (Ezekiel 34:4-5). The Good Shepherd has come to strengthen the weak, to heal the sick, to bind the wounds of the injured, to lead His people to green pastures and refreshing waters, to release the captives and to protect His flock (Ezekiel 34:11-16; Isaiah 61:1-9; Luke 4:18). This is the work of edification! As the Father sent the Son, so the Son has sent us (John 20:21)!

We are totally dependent upon the Spirit of God as we seek to fulfill the mission of our King (Zechariah 4:6). If Jesus required the anointing of the Spirit (Luke 4:18), how much more do we need to walk by the Spirit? We are asking the Spirit of God to show us what the Father is doing and saying (John 5:19-20), for we can do nothing of ourselves (John 15:5). We are asking, seeking and knocking for the Spirit (Luke 11:9-13). God alone is the One who can edify and meet needs, so we desire to lead others to Him.

When someone asks the cell for prayer, they are really coming to receive from God. The cell does not possess the answers or the healing edification. God alone is the source of what that person seeks. Our ministry as edifiers is to find out what God is doing and to bless that work.

Faulty Model #1 - The Psychiatrist Model

This model relies on going back to and digging up the past. This is the model which uses regression in order to find root causes. It assumes that healthy edification must begin by identifying that which happened in the past which is causing the present trouble.

Too many cells fall into this faulty model of edification as they seek to pray for one another week to week. Often there is a digging up of the past through excessive questioning of the one waiting to receive prayer. The information garnered in this way is then run through a filter developed from the "pop psychology" gleaned through the plethora of Christian self-help books on the shelves of Christian bookstores. Asking questions is not wrong in and of itself, but Christian "pop psychology" is best left outside the cell gathering.

The pastoral model, by way of contrast, relies on the Spirit and not on a method. We are not called to be psychiatrists. We are called to be ministers who follow the leading of the Lord. Edification deals with the past only as the Spirit leads and only when the Spirit requires. Multitudes are healed without knowing the specifics of their past. On the other hand, at times the Spirit may take someone back in order that they might deal with a past experience. If the psychiatrist model is employed as a method, it can do more harm than good by digging up that which the Spirit does not want to deal with at the moment.

Faulty Model #2 - The Authoritarian Model

This model employs a directive or authoritarian approach: "Here is your problem and this is what you must do about it." The authoritarian model communicates the idea of "I'm here to straighten you out. I have the answer."

When I was a child, I was amazed at how much my father knew and how wise he was. As a teenager, I became convinced my father's wisdom was outdated and needed to be updated, while my own wisdom was sufficient to answer life's questions, mine and others. As a young man newly married, I began to appreciate that my father knew some things I did not. The older I become, the more I realize how wise my father is and how little I know.

Too many cell members act like the teenager I described. They seem to think they have all the answers and view it as their job to straighten out everyone else. They speak with authority, even when they speak out of ignorance.

By contrast, the pastoral model seeks to be sensitive to the one seeking ministry. We are called to point those in need to the Lord, not to give our opinions or try to "fix" the one before us in need. That is the responsibility of the Holy Spirit. The person is wounded and needs to be handled with care. Yes, we do speak the truth; but we have been called alongside to facilitate health. Often, great healing occurs when the one seeking edification receives a revelation from God about the problem or solution. There is great value in loving a person, taking time to build the bridge of relationships and allowing God to restore them. Such a relational context is important to edification and is inherent in the cell.

Faulty Model #3- The Past Experience Model

As we live and minister, we begin to categorize our experiences. Sometimes, we dial up a past experience that is similar to the ministry situation in which we find ourselves. Then, we employ the method or techniques which worked in that similar circumstance to help this person. Permit a rather humorous illustration.

Joseph (fictitious name) came with a physical need to be met. He had intense pain in his neck and shoulder muscles. As we began to lay hands on Joseph and wait before the Lord for direction, the Lord said to inquire of Joseph regarding the relationship he had with his wife. We paused and asked Joseph how things were between he and his wife. Obviously, this would not have normally occurred to me. There is no apparent link between back pain and one's wife. Joseph began to confess that they had been fighting, He was angry and their relationship had gone sour the last few days. I asked Joseph if perhaps he thought the Lord wanted him to repent of his anger toward his wife. He agreed and began to confess and repent of his sins. When he was finished, he noticed that the pain in his neck and back had disappeared! So, what have we learned? The next time a man comes for prayer over his neck and shoulder pain, I dial up this past experience with Joseph and assume that his relationship with his wife is out of order, like Joseph's, he needs to repent and God will heal him. Never mind the man in front of me is single! I have dug into my past experience for the model of ministry today.

The pastoral model, in contrast, seeks to avoid casting ministry in the light of past experiences. Our past experiences are valid and can be used by God to enlighten our current work of edification. However, it is wrong to rely on what worked in a similar past situation. Jesus healed many blind people, but rarely in the same way. What past experience should He have relied upon? There was the spit-on-the-ground-make-clay-and-apply-to-the-eye-with-instructions-to-wash method (John 9:1-7). Then there was the spit-in-the-eye-and-lay-hands-on-and-pray method resulting in partial healing with a need for follow-up prayer (Mark 8:2-26). Then there was the overly simplistic touch-the-eyes-and-announce-healing-according-to-their-faith method (Matthew 9:27-30). Jesus did not fall back into a past experience for His model. He relied upon what the Spirit was showing at the moment. We are to rely on the Spirit, even as Jesus did. We need to get in on God's agenda, no matter how we may have categorized the need in the past. Remember, Jesus is the Master Edifier, not the group, nor you as an individual. He may or may not choose to work now as He did then!

Faulty Model #4 - The Parenting Model

The parenting model seeks to take responsibility for the individual in order to help or get them out of the mess in which they find themselves. Basically, this model infers that we can change the person. Some who come seeking ministry want others to make all the decisions for them, to be the source of meeting their needs. Christ alone must be the source.

The pastoral model, in contrast, seeks to lead people to the only One who can really meet their needs — Jesus. People must be led to take responsibility for themselves. A person will not be edified if they will not accept responsibility for their lives, obeying the leadership of the Holy Spirit for themselves. We must guard against the trap of taking the burden upon ourselves for changing the person or their situations. We must lead them to make responsible decisions for God, showing them how to rely on Him to meet their needs. Ultimately, the person may become angry with us when they discover we will not meet all of their needs.

How easy it is to slip into the parenting model! This is most deceptive. How often we gather around a person to pray for them. We ask of their need and immediately engage in prayer on their behalf. But wait! Would not God perhaps want them to take a first step. Perhaps they need to repent of sin. Perhaps they must forgive before a wounding can be prayed for. Perhaps the response God is calling them to is to confess their faith, or His greatness and ability. Perhaps they are to confess that they are embracing His sovereign ways in their life. Perhaps they ought to actively step out and reject a lie they have believed before we can break its power over their life. Perhaps they must choose by an act of their will against depression, anger, lust, or fear. We must never excuse them from personal responsibility for their life. We are not to pray *for* them, but *with* them. We are never to not pray *instead* of them, but like Hur and Aaron, we are to lift up their hands as they engage in the war in which they find themselves.

Conclusions

The pastoral model recognizes our role as undershepherds to the Chief Shepherd, Jesus Christ. Our task in edifying one another is to find out where He is leading and then lead the person there to encounter Him. We must learn to be patient and to wait on the Lord, not to rush ahead or venture into another pasture. Such haste usually leads us to employ a method rather than leading people to the Master. Our theme verse must be Isaiah 64:4: "God acts in behalf of the one who waits for Him."

Chapter 3 ☛ *Releasing Stereophonic Cell Ministry*

The Means of Edification

A key verse for understanding the means of edification is 1 Corinthians 12:7: "But to each one is given the manifestation of the Spirit for the common good." Within this short verse we find the when, who, how, and why of cell edification. We also find both poles of edification. The Spirit manifests, that is, He reveals Himself through His giftings. Each one of us is to receive His manifestation and minister His gifting for the common good.

When?

When might we expect edification to occur? Every time our cell comes together. "What is the outcome then, brethren? *When you assemble*, each one has a psalm, has a teaching, has a revelation, has a tongue, has an interpretation. Let all things be done for edification" (1 Corinthians 14:26). Each cell gathering is in effect an encounter, not a meeting. It is a time during which the cell members individually and collectively encounter the Living Presence of Christ, the Edifying Power of Christ, and the Ministering Purpose of Christ. 1 Corinthians 12:7 is clear. The manifestation of the Spirit *is being given*, present tense continuous action. It is Christ in the midst that allows edification to take place. We gather together in order to receive the work of His power in our lives, a work that we can not do for ourselves or for each other. We come together to posture ourselves in such a manner that He is able to edify us through one another.

Who?

Each member may become an instrument of edification. "But *to each one* is given the manifestation of the Spirit for the common good" (1 Corinthians 12:7). "What is the outcome then, brethren? When you assemble, each one has a psalm, has a teaching, has a revelation, has a tongue, has an interpretation" (1 Corinthians 14:26). It is the Christ who dwells in me that reaches out and touches others in the cell. It is not "super saints" who are used. Each cell member may be a vessel for honor, sanctified, useful to the Master, prepared for every good work (2 Timothy 2:21).

How?

Edification happens through the manifestation of the Spirit. "But to each one is given *the manifestation of the Spirit* for the common good. For to one is given the word of wisdom *through the Spirit*, and to another the word of knowledge *according to the same Spirit*; to another faith *by the same Spirit*, and to another gifts of healing *by the one Spirit*, and to another the effecting of miracles, and to another prophecy, and to another the distinguishing of spirits, to another various kinds of tongues, and to another the interpretation of tongues. But *one and the same Spirit works* all these things, distributing to each one individually just as He will" (1 Corinthians 12:7-11).

The Hand of God will touch one and then another, distributing to each one just as He wills that manifestation of grace to be employed by the Spirit in the building up of the individual and the cell as a whole. The manifestational giftings become the hands, the eyes and the mouth of God. In this manner God allows us to see through His eyes, touch with His hands, and speak with His voice.

Why?

Why does God release His gifts for edification? For the building up and common good of your cell. "What is the outcome then, brethren? When you assemble, each one has a psalm, has a teaching, has a revelation, has a tongue, has an interpretation. *Let all things be done for edification*" (1 Corinthians 14:26). As each one is given the manifestation of the Spirit, Christ's power flows through us, edifying, building up the cell and its members. Each one is given the manifestation of the Spirit for the common good. The Spirit is not manifested to show how spiritual we are. The Spirit is not manifested to show how mature we are. The Spirit is manifested for the well being of all present, and especially that "one" the Spirit may be focusing on for special ministry.

The Ministry of Edification

Cultivate Personal Sensitivity to the Holy Spirit

Become available as an Instrument of the Holy Spirit. God desires to use us and to pour Himself out through us that the Christ who dwells in us might touch others (Ephesians 2:10). We must cultivate an availability to be an instrument used of the Lord.

Start taking risks! It is one thing to believe God can use you; it is another thing to step out in faith and let Him use you. If you have a teachable heart, you are ready for God to instruct you. A posture of humility before the

Lord makes you ready to receive whatever He wants to give. If you are faithful in using the little, then He promises to give you much more (Matthew 25:23,29).

Deal ruthlessly with fear and doubt. Fear is a stronghold through which Satan can disarm you. If you harbor fear, then the shield of faith is lowered, exposing you to the missiles of the enemy (Ephesians 6:16). Fix your eyes on Jesus, not on your limitations as an instrument of edification. He is the author and finisher of your faith (Hebrews 2:2). Take captive thoughts of fear to the glory of Christ (2 Corinthians 10:5) as you focus on the demonstration of the Spirit's power (1 Corinthians 2:4-5).

Develop a sense of expectancy when you come together as a cell. God is on the move. Trust in the Holy Spirit to show up and do the works of Jesus through you (John 14:123-14). Ask the Spirit to open your eyes that you might see all the glorious things which He is doing.

Become willing to obey whatever the Holy Spirit shows. God will not give His direction to someone who will sit in judgment over what He says or does. We must deny ourselves, die to ourselves and follow Jesus (Luke 9:23). Following through in obedience to the will of the Lord will cause you to grow in the things of the Spirit. "If any man is willing to do His will he shall know if the teaching is from God" (John 7:17).

Become dependent upon God for His gifts. As we serve people, we are dependent upon the tools and resources which God provides. God's grace comes to us in terms of His gifts: words of knowledge and wisdom, faith, prophecy, mercy, etc. It is incumbent upon us to be sensitive and receptive to God's leading.

Become dependent upon God for His timing. We must let God show us when and how to reveal His direction. Every word of knowledge that comes does not necessarily need to be shared at that very moment. The Lord might actually be showing a person another issue and blurting out a word might interrupt what God is doing or get the edification process off-track. At times, God's graces and gifts should be shared if a blockage has been discovered. Often the words of knowledge will become the keys to identifying, defeating and overcoming obstacles to effective edification. Remember, the words still belong to God because they came from God. Be sensitive to the Spirit and share what He directs, as He directs, when He directs.

Cultivate Sensitivity to the One Needing Edification.

Create a safe environment. People who are hurting need love, acceptance and affirmation. It is very difficult to share about wounds and hurts. We need to be sensitive to this reality. When we begin to question the one we are seeking to edify, we must provide for them a haven of shelter. The sharing, therefore, must occur in a "safe place," a place in which the person feels affirmed and assured. It is beneficial for a cell to gather around a person receiving prayer and to lay hands upon them. The one receiving ministry will often benefit from a loving human touch, not to mention the spiritual dynamic of what is accomplished through the laying on of hands.

Confidentiality helps create a safe environment. Cell members will be more likely to feel safe and therefore open up when they know that what they are sharing will go no farther than the cell with whom they are sharing and the leaders who are responsible for their care However, recall that cell leaders, as extensions of pastoral ministry and functioning under delegated authority, have liberty to share with those to whom they are accountable.

Ask questions to determine what God is doing. The person seeking prayer is important in the edification process. Without their feedback, we would be incapable of knowing all that God is doing. We must encourage them to be honest. Ask them to share with you whatever they feel or sense, no matter how bizarre it might sound. Learn to listen both to the individual and the Holy Spirit at the same time.

Point the one being edified back to God. Just as important as feedback is the person's interaction with God. As God's help comes, it is helpful to let the person pray to Him. They need to be honest with God. Encourage them to share their hurts, fears and prayers of confession to God. Their prayers will reveal to you much of what is going on in their mind and heart. Are they mad at God? Do they have a poor understanding of God's love? Are they able to be honest? As people open up to God, they are able to receive from Him (Revelation 3:20). As they pray, do you sense any breakthrough? Remember, God is here and wants to meet the needy. Introduce them to one another. Ask God to loose His gifts of repentance and confession so that the person might act on God's present grace. The one seeking edification must take personal responsibility before God, or else edification and freedom will not come.

DIVINE REVELATION -
DEALING WITH ROOTS NOT FRUITS

God's work of edification is a process. God uses the edification process to deal with our sins, hurts, pains, conflicts, anger and emotional needs to bring about a building up in our life and the life of the Body. Each of the steps in the edification process is necessary for the next step to take place.

Step #1: Identification

Step number one in the edification process is identification. Understanding, naming and defining specifically both the fruit and root of my pain, anger, hurt and/or conflict is the starting place. The cell is like a garden where Jesus is able to cultivate and produce good fruit in the individual Christian. In so doing, He then ultimately builds up the cell itself. Christ produces good fruit in us by giving special attention to the factors that produce it – the roots. From healthy root edification grows good spiritual fruit.

The Lord does His work of edification at the point of our attitudes, feelings, emotions, strongholds, fleshly desires, unconfessed sin, and unhealed wounds. We too often avoid such roots and settle for ministry at a surface level by dealing with the multitude of circumstances and fruits that grow out of a diseased root. Our fruits are such things as our pains, hurts, perceived needs, problems, relationships, behavior, actions, and incidents.

If a cell is to enter into spiritual edification, the members must be willing for Christ to do whatever is necessary to heal the roots and not just the fruits in their lives.

Why is it so difficult to identify root causes of our sins and hurts? We may be walking in *denial*. Identifying the real causes of our hurts, pains and sins may be too painful. Thus, we deny their existence. A loving community is often God's means of moving us out of denial and into truth and reality. The cause may be deeply buried within us. We may honestly not know the real causes of the destructive fruit in our life. The root causes may be buried so deeply in childhood or unresolved events in the past that we are blind to them.

We may be living in *deception*. The problem may be spiritual blindness. We may have a spiritual stronghold where a series of hurts and pains intermesh and interrelate. That network of sins, feelings and habits that Satan has built into one spiritual stronghold prevents us from "seeing" the real root.

We may have an unhealthy *dependence* upon another person. We may be dependent upon another person to the extent that we are unable to really identify and deal with our own hurts, feelings and sins. Satan may have drawn us into such an unhealthy co-dependent relationship with someone else (wife, husband, child, father, mother, etc.) that we cannot come to grips with ourselves. Not only do we carry all our own feelings, pains, hurts and sins, but we also carry those of the other person.

God desires to identify the roots of the sins, conflicts, feelings and hurts (fruits) in our lives before He begins to edify us or our cell. Identification involves our seeing the roots as God sees them. King David was a "man after God's own heart" because he recognized the importance of honestly facing the truth before God about himself. David recognized a truth that would become a spiritual principle in the New Testament. It is necessary for God to identify our sins before we can either rightly relate to Him or be used by Him. He understood that identification of our sins and needs must come before our edification. "Search me, O God, and know my heart; Try me and know my anxious thoughts; And see if there be any hurtful way in me, And lead me in the everlasting way" (Psalm 139:23-24). Remember, God reveals roots primarily through revelation, not reason. Don't fall into the trap of trying to "figure it out"!

The starting point for edification is the identification process. Since the edification process begins at the point of identification, only after God has identified the real root causes of that which tears us apart instead of building us up are we in a position and condition to allow His edification to take place in our own lives. Only as we listen to God and receive revelation from Him concerning the root will we be able to truly build up one another. When we seek edification without first asking God to search and know us, we sidestep a vital stepping stone on the pathway toward genuine edification.

Step #2: Confession

Step two in the edification process is confession. Confession is acknowledging, verbalizing, owning what has been identified as the root causes and sources of my pain, anger, hurt and/or conflict.

Confession means acknowledgement. It means putting a face and a name to what Satan wants to cover up by one big blob of hurt, pain, anger or bitterness. It means giving definition to that mass of problems we have lumped together that causes us confusion, overwhelms us and deceives us. It means getting specific rather than living and talking and praying in generalities.

Our confession is not a mental agreement with what man has spoken to us, however correct man may be. Genuine confession flows from our agreement with what God has spoken to our heart. It is only after we acknowledge God's revelation that we will confess our roots and move toward genuine change. Our confession to one another in cell life moves us one step closer towards edification and healing. "Therefore confess your sins to one another, and pray for one another, so that you may be healed. The effective prayer of a righteous man can accomplish much" (James 5:16).

DECISIVE TRANSFORMATION - WHEN IS A DOOR NOT A DOOR?

Step #3: **Renovation**

The third step in the edification process is what I call renovation. Renovation is defined as, "to begin again; to resume; to restore to life, vigor, activity; to revive; to regenerate; to renew, to make over, or repair; to restore to freshness, purity, a sound state". Renovation commences as I actually begin to change in my life what I have identified as destructive, dysfunctional and sinful attitudes and actions and begin walking in the "mind of Christ".

Riddles are hidden sayings solved by guessing. Perhaps the most famous from the Bible is the riddle Samson posed to the men of Ashkelon in Judges 14:12-19. There are, however, often kernels of wisdom wrapped inside a riddle. For example, take the old riddle, "When is a door not a door?" The answer is obvious, when its ajar (a jar). What, you wonder, does that have to do with the process of edification and especially renovation? It really is at the heart of edification and the reason why so much "edification" is continually ineffective in the lives of cell members. A door is not a door when it is something else, a jar. Only when the door has been transformed into a jar is it no longer a door.

Perhaps a few other questions may shed greater light. When is a liar no longer a liar? When he stops lying? Far from it. He may have stopped simply because it suits his needs. His mouth may be taped shut. There are endless reasons why he may have stopped. But does that make him no longer a liar? No. When is a thief no longer a thief? The obvious answer, and incorrect response, is when he stops stealing. However, he may be in jail. He may have enough for the present.

A liar is no longer a liar when he lays aside falsehood and begins to speak truth. A thief is no longer a thief when he gets a job, begins to work, and then shares with others from that which he now has earned. This is Paul's testimony in Ephesians 4:25-28. Change, renovation, is always a two factored process, a "putting off" and a corresponding "putting on".

To "put off" and then to "put on" the corresponding biblical alternative, to head in one direction and then change 180 degrees and travel in the other direction, this is the essence of true repentance. This is the key to permanent transformation and a step toward lasting edification.

Put Off	Put On
Ephesians 4:22 Strip yourselves of your former nature — **put off and discard your old unrenewed self** — which characterized your previous manner of life and becomes corrupt through lusts and desires that spring from delusion; (Amplified Version)	**Ephesians. 4:23-24** And be constantly renewed in the spirit of your mind — having a fresh mental and spiritual attitude; **And put on the new nature** [the regenerate self] created in God's image, [Godlike] in true righteousness and holiness.
Colossians 3:9 **Do not lie to one** another, since you **laid aside the old self** with its evil practices,	**Colossians 3:10-11** and have **put on the new self** who is being renewed to a true knowledge according to the image of the One who created him -- a renewal in which there is no distinction between Greek and Jew, circumcised and uncircumcised, barbarian, Scythian, slave and freeman, but Christ is all, and in all.

Chapter 3 ☛ *Releasing Stereophonic Cell Ministry*

DELIBERATE RENOVATION - RE-BUILDING BY A DIVINE PLUMBLINE

The most vital issues of life arise out of the heart (Proverbs 4:23). God has extended the plumbline of His Word alongside the hearts of those He has called to be His people. For a fuller treatment of the concept of the divine plumbline and its relationship to our heart, I refer the reader to Dr. Bruce Thompson's work, *The Walls of My Heart*, available through Youth With a Mission.

In the 8th century B.C., during the reign of Uzziah, King of Judah, the nation of Israel was being carried along on the wings of prosperity and peace. Along with this affluence came a rapid decline in morals. Social injustice obscured Israel's view and it lost its divinely given direction. Into this arena of life God called Amos, a shepherd and dresser of fig trees. While with Moses God chose a rod to demonstrate His truth and values, with Amos God chose to use a plumbline.

A plumbline in its simplest form is a small inverted cone of lead, attached by a cord to a cylindrical piece of wood of the same diameter. It is used by builders to ascertain the precise vertical direction for the construction of a wall. If a building is to be stable and not topple down, its studs and walls must line up with the plumbline.

Realizing that we build defensive walls around our heart, walls that become our own personal prison, God extends the plumbline of HIs Word alongside our hearts today. Just as a building inspector uses a plumbline to ensure that a structure is safe to be in, so God uses the divine plumbline to evaluate the building of our lives. The measure to which our lives are out of line with His standards reflects the degree of insecurity, instability and vulnerability we feel in life. Whereas identification is learning our lives have been built out of plumb and confession is acknowledging our shoddy workmanship, renovation is moving our lives back in line with His plumbline.

Renovation begins as we allow God to tear down the old out-of-plumb walls we have built into our life (Ezekiel 13:15-16). "And the high fortifications of your walls [the Lord] will bring down, lay low, and bring to the ground, even to the dust" (Amplified Version, Isaiah 25:12). God often uses storms to assail our walls and reveal to us how out of plumb and tottering they really are. These storms are often financial, marital, health or even career. The old must be first torn down and the rubble removed before a new wall can be built.

Renovation continues as together we build the new walls of salvation. "In that day shall this song be sung in the land of Judah: We have a strong city; [the Lord] sets up salvation as walls and bulwarks" (Amplified Version, Isaiah 26:1). "But you will call your walls salvation, and your gates praise" (NASB, Isaiah 60:18b).

LASTING EDIFICATION

As "lively stones" we are taken from the quarry of the world to be built into a dwelling of God through the Spirit. We have to be cut and shaped, hewn and measured, and then fitted together corporately. All believers are involved in this building process according to the measure of the grace-gifts given to them by Christ and the power of the Holy Spirit (I Corinthians 3:9; Romans 12:1-8).

Why then do people come week after week to cell with the same needs, request the same ministry, experience the same spiritual feelings, yet leave with the same problems surfacing the next morning when they awake? Could it be a result of not following through with the edification process? Could it be that they may have received revelation regarding their roots, even confessed them with tears of genuine repentance, yet have not entered into the two-factored process of renovation, and thus have failed to bring their lives into line with God's plumbline and effect permanent change?

As stereophonic cell ministry is released and we move through the entire process of identification, confession and renovation, genuine and lasting edification will be the inevitable result. The release of prophetic giftings as those in our cell pray for us will build us up together in Him (I Corinthians 14:3-5, 12). As we experience the love of God flowing through the people of God, together we will be built up (I Corinthians 8:1). With sin released, the resultant peace and harmony of the Lord will build us up (Romans 14:9; Matthew 5:3-12). As our lives are brought into plumb with God's life within and we put off the destructive patterns that have dominated our lives, replacing them with their biblical alternative, we become more deeply rooted and grounded in the faith,. and the Great Architect, Jesus, is able to complete His entire process of edification, building us, His house, and making us a glorious living edifice, a holy habitation for Himself through the Spirit.

RELEASING STEREOPHONIC CELL MINISTRY

The New Testament is replete with texts exhorting us to edify one another and/or be built up (Romans 14:19; Romans 15:2; 1 Corinthians 14:12; Ephesians 2:22; Ephesians 4:12; Ephesians 4:29; Colossians 2:71; Thessalonians 5:11; 1 Peter 2:5; Jude 1:20). As previously noted, edification is the guiding principle of cell life. There is one rule which applies to everything which happens within the basic Christian community, the cell. Everything must serve to build up the community (1 Corinthians 14:12, 17, 26; Romans 14:19; 15:2; 1 Thessalonians 5:11; Ephesians 4:29). Thus the gifts of grace and offices are judged according to what they contribute to the building up of the community (1 Corinthians 14:3-5; Ephesians 4:29), not according to mere spiritual experience.

Viewing edification through bipolar lenses will help us maintain our balance in this delicate partnership between the work of Jesus and our part in the process of edification. Walking the bipolar path will keep us in dynamic partnership with Jesus, and keep us from falling either into the right ditch of monism where we expect edification to happen if we use the right formulas and say the right words and maintain the right rituals, or falling into the left ditch of dualism where we simply wash our hands and leave it all up to the sovereign work of the Holy Spirit, assuming we have no part but to receive, and no responsibility after the Spirit does His work.

Edification is one of those things that cannot fully take place outside the realm of Christian community. As the basic Christian community, the cell is the most obvious place for mutual edification to occur. When we apply the bipolarity of Natural Church Development to our cell edification, we come away with a winning combination–a win-win scenario for cell church and NCD.

4

GROWING STEREOPHONIC CELL CHURCHES

FOR THE BODY IS NOT ONE MEMBER, BUT MANY...IF THE WHOLE BODY WERE AN EYE, WHERE WOULD THE HEARING BE? IF THE WHOLE WERE HEARING, WHERE WOULD THE SENSE OF SMELL BE? BUT NOW GOD HAS PLACED THE MEMBERS, EACH ONE OF THEM, IN THE BODY, JUST AS HE DESIRED. IF THEY WERE ALL ONE MEMBER, WHERE WOULD THE BODY BE?   1 CORINTHIANS 12:14, 17-19

Chapter 4 — Growing Stereophonic Cell Churches

THE BIPOLAR NATURE OF THE CHURCH - INTEGRATING AN EPHESIAN ECCLESIOLOGY

Too often, when attempting to understand the nature of the church, our tendency is to develop an understanding primarily from the book of Acts. While Acts may give us the best picture of the work of the Holy Spirit both in the Apostles and in the new church, Acts alone is rather incomplete to show us the very nature of the New Testament church. For this reason, I am suggesting we look further, and delve into Paul's letter to the church at Ephesus to help gain a fuller understanding.

When Paul describes the church in his letter to the Ephesians, he employs a number of organic as well as inorganic metaphors to describe a living organism. He calls the church "a holy temple in the Lord" (2:21 an inorganic metaphor), "a dwelling of God" (2:22 an inorganic metaphor), and "the body of Christ" (4:12 an organic metaphor). Paul also informs us that the church is "the fullness of God (1:23 an organic metaphor), God's workmanship (2:10 an inorganic metaphor), and the whole building of God (2:21 an inorganic metaphor)." From this we can begin to see the bipolar nature of the church. What conclusions can we draw?

First, the church as an organism is, by definition, living. Adam became alive when God breathed His breath into him (Genesis 2:7). When this breath left him, his body was nothing more than an empty shell. The life of the Spirit is much more crucial than the structures of men. We need to organize the church, but if God does not breathe His breath of life into that organization, our organizational structures will exist in vain. We will have nothing but an empty shell. Correct church organization does not guarantee that the life of the Spirit will be present.

Second, because the church is a living body, it must always be in a process of growth. All organisms grow and reproduce. To do otherwise is to be consigned to death. Paul wrote that the church is "growing into a holy temple in the Lord" (2:21). Note Paul's joining of both organic and inorganic metaphors–growing temple. He goes on to state that "we are to grow up in all aspects into Him who is the head, even Christ, from whom the whole body, being fitted and held together by what every joint supplies, according to the proper working of each individual part, causes the growth of the body for the building up of itself in love" (4:15-16). Note once again Paul's use of organic "growth" coupled with inorganic architectural "building". Because the church is in a process of growth (organic aspect), it should be flexible in terms of methods and structures (organizational aspect). We might even go so far as to say that the church, as a living organism, demands an organizational structure that is capable of keeping up with its growth and change. To be inflexible structurally would stifle and ultimately kill the life of the church.

The church is also an inorganic organization with a defined structure. The "saints" of verse 19 have been "built" on the foundation of the apostles and prophets of verse 20. Yet, in Paul's view, this inorganic church possesses organic qualities. We see in verse 21 that "the whole building…is growing into a holy temple". Paul has painted for us a picture of a structure that requires organized planning and yet demands spontaneous life at the same time, a constant interchange between human administration and divine inspiration. Broadly speaking, a structure may be defined as being composed of any number of different parts which have been purposefully assembled in a particular design in order to form a whole. In the same way, the church is a structure which consists of individual people with varying ministry offices and gifts who are being assembled according to God's design in order to form the body of Christ in the earth for the praise of His glory (1:6, 11, 14; 4:11–16). Ephesians 2:19–22 again describes the structure of the church as both organic and inorganic, spontaneous and planned.

Ephesians 2:19–22 and 4:15–16 offer four principles which describe the basic structure of the church and the process by which it grows: 1) every member is connected both directly and indirectly to Christ; 2) as the head, Christ is solely responsible for the growth of the body; 3) the health of the body is the responsibility of every individual member; and 4) the body is responsible to build itself up in love.

While the whole body is "being held together and fitted by what every joint supplies" (4:16), each member is immediately connected to Christ, who is the Head. This truth is echoed in 2:20–21 by the image of Christ as the "corner stone," upon which the "whole building" is being built. Just as every stone is supported by the primary corner stone, so every member of the body is immediately connected to the strength which Christ supplies. At the same time, Paul addresses his audience in Ephesus as "fellow citizens with the saints" who have been built on the "foundation of the apostles and prophets" (2:19–20). Paul wants his Gentile audience to understand their need of both Christ and the saints, i.e. their dependence upon Christ, whether directly from the head or indirectly from those in the body. In a body, the various members need not only the head, but also each other. If the church is to become what the Lord intends it to be, each member must acknowledge their own dependence upon the other members. Paul not only instructed the Ephesians to grow up "into Him" (4:15), but also to become "fitted together" and "built together" (4:21-22). Note the organic concept of community. The whole body is held together by what every joint supplies.

Because Christ is responsible for the growth of every believer, He is ultimately responsible for the growth of the entire body. Believers have been chosen "in Him before the foundation of the world" (1:4), "predestined...to adoption as sons through Jesus Christ" (1:5), "sealed in Him with the Holy Spirit of promise" (1:13), "made...alive together with Christ" (2:5), and "raised...up with Him, and seated...with Him in the heavenly places in Christ" (2:6). This work of Christ is done by grace through faith so that no one can boast about bringing growth to the body by his own personality, planning, leadership skills or creativity (2:8–9).

Even though growth is ultimately Christ's responsibility, He has put the responsibility of the health of the body in the hands of every member. In other words, as every member contributes to the body's overall health, God will be faithful to cause the body to grow. Beginning with the cornerstone, good health is transferred to the body through "the foundation of the apostles and prophets" (2:19), i.e., the church leadership. This transference of knowledge, leadership and power is the starting point of the church's ministry to the rest of the body and the world. In Ephesians 4:11-13, Paul names five gifted individuals who have been given to the body for the purpose of "equipping the saints for the work of service, to the building up of the body of Christ, until we all attain to the unity of the faith, and of the knowledge of the Son of God, to a mature man, to the measure of the stature which belongs to the fullness of Christ."

The goal of Christian leadership is to equip those under their charge for ministry and to bring them to their full potential in Christ. This equipping is vital for every believer, not just a few, or even just the majority, because the body of Christ is held together "by what every joint supplies, according to the proper working of each individual part" (4:16). Paul warned the church in Corinth not to favor any gifts more than others (1 Corinthians 12:15-25). 1 Peter 4:10 states, "As each one has received a special gift, employ it in serving one another as good stewards of the manifold grace of God." It takes variety to express "the manifold Grace of God." Every member equipped for ministry it not an option - it is a premise for a functional body

Because the body is responsible for the transference of leadership and the work of the ministry, it follows that it is also responsible to build itself up in love. But this responsibility does not come without divine aid, for Paul states clearly that this work of self-edification is preceded by the growth which is provided by Christ Himself: "(God) causes the growth of the body for the building up of itself in love" (4:16). The NIV says it this way: "From him the whole body, joined and held together by every supporting ligament, grows and builds itself up in love, as each part does its work." The analogy of a body is used here to add to the picture of a corporate organism made up of small little individual organs and muscles each doing their part. Each part has a responsibility to ensure growth and survival. The lifestyle and gifts of each member should focus on building one another up.

The church is able to fulfill the purpose of Christ because of the utilization of the diversity of spiritual gifts given by His Spirit. The operation of the diverse gifts of the Spirit requires holiness in the life of every believer. We can maintain unity within this diversity (4:3) because the gifts function to work towards the building up of the body of Christ and to prepare all believers for works of service (4:12). The ability of the church to attaining the fullness of Christ mentioned above revolves around our ability to maintain unity through the operation of the gifts of His Spirit (4:13).

It is important to recognize that this ministry is for the edification of the church at large. Just as each organ of the body is working for the good of the overall body, so each member of Christ's body is working for the good of the whole. This understanding is crucial to the use for the gifts in ministry. Without this, there will be rampant misuse of the gifts, and what was meant to be a beautiful unity will become selfish chaos.

Obviously, what has preceded is but a brief overview of Paul's Ephesian ecclesiology. However, if we agree we must embrace a bipolar paradigm of the church as both by nature an organization and an organism, then whatever inorganic structure we develop must of necessity reflect and stimulate to further development that organic nature of the church as the Body of Christ. This has major consequences for the full blown development of a cell church, and not only challenges our current structures, but also our very reliance upon a cell/celebration paradigm for cell church development.

Chapter 4 ☛ *Growing Stereophonic Cell Churches*

THE PROBLEM WITH CELLS AND CELEBRATION

The Problem Defined

When one reads the extant literature regarding the development of cell churches, one can only come away with the understanding that cell churches have cells, celebration services, and facilitative functions, that is, the necessary elements of church life that do not directly fit into the ministry of cell groups. Upon further inspection, these facilitative functions almost entirely fit into what happens during the celebration services. This cell church paradigm is a far cry from the Church described by Paul to the Ephesian saints. It seems rather to be a church comprised of a head with interconnecting cells. What is lacking is a body! I'm being too harsh, you argue? Examine with me representative excerpts from the literature and compare them with the picture of the Church that Paul painted in Ephesians and Corinthians.

In their exceptional work, *Cell Church Planter's Guide*, Bob Logan and Jeannette Buller summarize and reflect back to the reader this cell church paradigm. It should be noted that Logan and Buller are merely assisting the reader in understanding the current paradigm, they are not blazing new trails. Logan and Buller, having listed seven classic books on cell church, write:

> Understanding from books such as these is essential in the reading and use of this manual. Because we are focusing on church planting, we will not take much time to expound on the cell church paradigm in general, which has been adequately explored in these other books. (Cell, vii)

They provide (Cell, 1-6) the reader with the following summary of the cell-celebration church paradigm:

> Cell groups are disciple-making communities. A network of reproducing cell groups that gather regularly for celebration and worship is called a cell-celebration church. The unique characteristic of a cell church is that the foundational building blocks of the life of the church are the cell groups rather than committees, task groups, or Sunday morning services.

They continue by enumerating 12 ministry principles that define the cell-celebration paradigm (Cell, 1-7). These are listed below:

1. **Integration** – Disciple-making small groups are the basic building blocks of the church.

2. **3-Fold Function** – Healthy cell groups fulfill a three-fold function of evangelism, pastoral care, and leadership development.

3. **Community** – True Christian community, nurtured primarily through cell groups, creates an environment that welcomes newcomers and encourages personal growth. All members are part of a cell group and are experiencing cell life.

4. **Compassion for the Harvest** – Lost people matter to God, and the church understands its role in reaching the harvest.

5. **Leadership Development** – Leadership development through apprenticing, training, and coaching is a primary role of the church's leadership.

6. **Division of Labor** – Pastoral lay leaders are allowed to lead, and members are given the work of the ministry.

7. **Multiplication** – The cell groups are designed with the ability to multiply as they grow in size.

8. **Mobilizing Spiritual Gifts** – A deeper understanding of spiritual gifts mobilizes the laity in ministry.

9. **Spiritual Development** – New Christians need to be discipled so they can grow spiritually and become productive Kingdom builders.

10. **Celebrations** – The gathering of the cells together for cel-

ebration is vital to the health of the cells and the growth of the church.

11. **Obedience** – Being the church that God has called us to be is more important than holding on to traditions.

12. **Prayer** – Prayer forms the foundation for the life and growth of the church.

While the celebrations are mentioned, corporate Body life outside of a weekly meeting is sadly absent from the principles that define the cell-celebration church paradigm. But remember, Logan and Buller are simply reflecting back what the cell church movement has already propounded.

Making Cell Groups Work by Scott Boren devotes and entire section, three chapters, to the development and establishment of what the author calls "the hidden systems that support cells. (323)" The author, in summarizing the importance of stage 7 writes:

> In stage 7, it is time to answer the question, "How do we establish cell groups as the basis of the church?" In other words, this is the period when the church will look to restructure the church organization to support the cell groups properly. (324)

If we are indeed looking to restructure the church organization (static pole) to support cell groups (I assume by *support* the author's intention is to release the life of Christ, i.e. stimulate the dynamic pole), one would assume the issues of body life vis-a-vis Ephesians and Corinthians would be addressed. Unfortunately, that is not the case. Section 7.3 will deal with options for incorporating children into cells. Section 7.2 will deal with the issue of establishing pastoral oversight. Section 7.1, "Establish a Critical Mass," is the only section dealing at all with what the author terms "subsystems (326). In obtaining critical mass, he discusses critical mass conviction (326-327), critical mass sub-systems (327-332), and critical mass spirituality (332-337). Turn your attention with to what he writes regarding these critical mass sub-systems. Boren writes:

> These sub-systems are often unseen and therefore easy to

ignore. Cell groups will not grow and multiply without the necessary support systems, just as ships cannot move along the ocean without the hundreds of unseen parts that hold them together and allow the sails to catch the wind. Stage 1 introduced the macro view of the cell based model, which illustrates how the major components of the system work together. But at this point, it is necessary to understand the sub-systems from a more detailed point of view. In order to reach critical mass, all of the sub-systems must be in place. (Making, 327-328)

On page 328 of *Making Cell Groups Work*, Boren goes on to enumerate the following eleven parallel sub-systems:

1. Practicing the Great Commandment and the Great Commission in the cell groups.

2. Celebrating God's presence as a corporate church

3. Providing pastoral oversight to cell groups

4. Providing coaches for every cell group leader

5. Cell member equipping developed

6. Regular training provided for new cell leaders

7. Excellent on-going cell leader support meetings provided

8. Providing training and opportunities for relationship evangelism

9. Incorporating children into cell group vision

10. Incorporating youth into cell vision

11. Establishing clear system for facilitative functions

In reference to the eleventh sub-system on the list, what are the facilitative functions for which clear systems are to be developed? "Facilitative functions are the necessary elements of church life that do not directly fit into the ministry of cell groups. They include the organization of church-wide prayer events, oversight of corporate evangelism thrusts, provision of corporate children's ministry, care of the children in the nursery, ad service as greeters or ushers during celebration. (Making, 330)" Notice that each of these facilitative functions is either tied to the celebrative services or are event oriented. Boren later writes of cell groups assuming the "different responsibilities of the corporate church" and notes such corporate responsibilities as greeting on Sunday, parking cars on Sunday, and serving in the nursery on Sunday (Making, 331).

While writing that the "facilitative functions are necessary for a church to operate properly" (Making 331), one should note the author's underlying assumption when he also writes that "serving in these functions is a great way to help people grow in their leadership responsibilities before they enter into cell leadership training. (Making, 332). The author proceeds in the next section to refer back to what has been written earlier as "biblical structure. (Making, 332)"

If the Whole Body were an Eye, Where would the Hearing Be?

In Romans chapter 12 and 1 Corinthians chapter 12, Paul paints a far different portrait of the church as the Body of Christ.

In Romans 12, Paul begins by writing of our own physical body with its many members. There is unity in the midst of diversity among our members (one body — many members). He goes on to state that the members of our body do not all have the same function. Our members possess differing functionality. The word translated "function" is the Greek *praxis*. In Acts 19:18 and Colossians 3:9 it is translated as "practices". The term denotes a doing, transaction, a deed the action of which is looked upon as incomplete and in progress. This can be contrasted with *pragma*, that which has been done, an accomplished act. Each member of the human body has a function that is continually going on and will be in progress until the death of the body sets in. Each member is set in the body with a responsibility, a specific function.

Christ also has but one Body, though composed of many members. His Body also possesses unity in the midst of diversity. One Body — many members. All the members of Christ's Body do not possess the same gifts of grace. These charismata are given according to God's charis (grace).

The charismata is not so much a "thing possessed" as it is a "responsibility expressed". We have gifts of grace, charismata, that differ according to the grace given to us, according to our appointed tasks within the Body of Christ. Appointed tasks arise out of received gifts.

Charismata is a power term. God's grace is His power flowing through the believer to other believers to edify the Body (2 Corinthians 12:9ff). God's grace demonstrates itself in fruit (our character) and gifts (edifying others), touching others with God's power.

Thus, as in the human body, this charismata denotes a doing, transaction, a deed the action of which is looked upon as incomplete and in progress. Again, in similar fashion each member of Christ's Body has a function that continues as long as there is life. Each member of Christ's Body is set in place with a specific responsibility, a specific function. Every member of the Body of Christ is a minister!

Paul expresses similar thoughts to the Corinthian church throughout 1 Corinthians 12:1-27. The human body is one (12). There is unity within the body. Yet there are many members comprising the body. Once again there is diversity within unity (12). The body is not one member, but many. God created each member of the body as He desired, whether the foot, the hand, the ear, the eye or the nose. He created each member possessing differing functionality. The eye does not perform the same function as the ear. If the whole were just one member, where would the body be? God has placed each member in the body as He desired. Each member is vital for the others. Only as each member functions correctly will the body corporately function correctly. "But now there are many members, but one body".

In the spiritual, there is one Body. "So also is Christ" (12). One Body in unity with many members in diversity. Paul says to the Corinthian church, "Now you are Christ's Body, and individually members of it." All the members have been appointed by God, placed by God in the Body as He desired. All have differing gifts. All possess differing functionality in any local setting. Only as each member functions correctly will the Body corporately function correctly.

Paul is unmistakably clear when he states in verse 14, "For the body is not one member, but many. "How can our current cell-celebration church paradigm answer Paul's questions in verses 17 and 19? "If the whole body

Chapter 4 ☛ *Growing Stereophonic Cell Churches*

were an eye, where would the hearing be? If the whole were hearing, where would the sense of smell be...and if they were all one member, where would the body be?" Paul never envisioned congregations of cells (what has been described as "working spiritual units that help enable cell leaders and cells to 'do the work of ministry', and "where every task of the church comes alive in dynamic cell life") covered by a huge flexible celebration skin. That is not a picture of a body, but of interconnected blobs of protoplasm somehow stuffed into a large skin. Would we be out of order to re-phrase the beginning of Paul's question and ask, "If the whole body were cell leaders, G12 leaders and coaches, where would the rest of the body be?"

Let me suggest that cell and celebration are not parallel terms. We might speak about a cell *meeting* and a celebration *service*. Now we are speaking merely about two *events* on two days. We might speak about a *lifestyle* lived on two planes, a *lifestyle* within the small Christian community and a larger corporate community *lifestyle*. Now we are speaking about two *lifestyles* lived 24/7. But to define a cell church in terms of a lifestyle lived within a small Christian community (cell) and an event attended once a week (celebration) is to mix and match apples and oranges. It is to limit our Christian lifestyle to simply the cell plane, and ignore the fact that the Body of Christ has a corporate existence to be experienced, and we are, as members of that Body, graced with spiritual gifts, to live out our Christian life on that corporate level also.

The cells in my natural body may have a small group experience every day, but they do not gather once a week to form my body. There is a corporate nature to my body that all my cells take part in and contribute to on a moment by moment basis. In fact, the whole is greater than the sum of the parts. That is the nature of a complex organism, as opposed to a single celled amoeba.

Is it possible that in our zeal to avoid remaining a program-based design church we have over reacted? As a consequence of lacking a corporate paradigm, cell churches have often stumbled headlong into the pit of "program denigration". Some cell churches pride themselves on no longer having "programs", only "ministries". However, to paraphrase and apply Mr. Shakespeare, a program by any other name is still a program. Programs are neither intrinsically nor inherently evil. If we truly have become a values-driven cell church, then our values will determine our usage of time, energy and resources (our priorities), what key skills we emphasize (our practices), and how we engage in ministry (our programs). Our programs are no more and no less than the structures, forms, and vehicles which we use to minister (serve) to those around us. What distinguishes a cell church from a program-based design church is not whether or not programs exist, but whether the programs have been created at the top and imposed downward, or whether the programs have been allowed to develop from the bottom upward. Where they have been permitted to develop from the ground up, they are expressions of values and the result of God's people giving expression to divine giftings. They are therefore functional and not sacred. They can be started, changed, or discontinued at any time.

Our current cell-celebration church paradigm is inadequate. It addresses lifestyle on an intimate small group level, but makes little or no provision for allowing us to live out our Christian life 24/7 on a corporate level and contribute to the growth and development of the whole body through the employment of our spiritual giftings, apart from celebration services or other ad hoc events. It must be redefined.

Having pointed out that the Emperor really has on no clothes, I do not wish to have him remain naked. In the sections that follow I will suggest how we may obtain a tailor made suit to clothe his nakedness.

DEVELOPING A VALUES-DRIVEN ORGANIC OPERATING SYSTEM

Preparing the 21st Century Church introduced the reader to the concepts of value propositions, value disciplines, and values-driven operating models as they relate to the development of a cell church. It is time to build upon that introduction and see how Natural Church Development can help us build a values-driven operating system to clothe the nakedness of the Emperor.

Embracing Your Value Discipline

A bit of a review would be in order here. Let's begin by reviewing some definitions (Preparing, 158-160):

Value Proposition

The implicit promise a church makes to both its members and target community to deliver a particular combination of values. In the case of a church, as opposed to that of a business, the "customers" who were originally identified as the target community may eventually become members of the church itself. Additionally, the "customers" who in fact are the church members, are not really "customers" at all, but instead part of the very "business". This understanding will prove helpful when examining the value discipline of Customer Intimacy.

Value Disciplines

The three desirable ways in which churches can combine operating models and value propositions so as to excel. Each discipline hones at least one component of value to a level of excellence that puts other churches to shame. Choosing to pursue a value discipline is not like choosing to pursue a strategic goal. One cannot simply graft a value discipline on to or integrate it into a church's normal existing philosophy. The selection of a value discipline is a central act that shapes every subsequent plan and decision a church makes, coloring the entire church organization/organism, from its competencies to its culture. The choice of a value discipline defines what a church does and, to some degree, what a church is.

Values-Driven Operating Model

Operating models are made up of operating processes, church structure, management systems, and culture, all of which are synchronized to create a certain superior value and give a church the capacity to create unsurpassed value and to deliver on its value proposition. If the value proposition is the end, the value-driven operating model is the means to the end. Different value disciplines demand different operating models.

Delivering unsurpassed, ever improving value requires a superior, dedicated operating model. The church must build a well-tuned **values-driven operating model dedicated to delivering unmatched value**. The operating model is the key. How can this be accomplished? Consider the following.

God causes the Church to grow. One need only examine in some detail Mark 4:26-29 to become persuaded of this.

> And He was saying, "The kingdom of God is like a man who casts seed upon the soil; and goes to bed at night and gets up by day, and the seed sprouts up and grows-- how, he himself does not know. The soil produces crops by itself; first the blade, then the head, then the mature grain in the head. But when the crop permits, he immediately puts in the sickle, because the harvest has come."

What a man can do is sow and harvest, sleep and rise. What a man cannot do is to bring forth the fruit. "The soil produces crops by itself" (Mark 4:28 αυτοματη γαρ η γη καρποφορει). The Greek αυτοματη, by itself, is the derivation of our word automate. Unlike our current thinking, the underlying thought in Hebraic thinking is that what is observed to be automatic is in fact being performed by God. Thus, fruit or crops that develop seemingly automatically by themselves are in reality a work of God.

The church must be thought of as an organism. All living things grow. God has placed within each living thing a growth dynamic. Yet, we must not relegate that growth dynamic to an impersonal growth principle, a rather Deistic approach. No, we must see that growth as being performed by God. Growth is in reality a work of God. The question then becomes how to release the very life God has placed within the church so that it can grow "all by itself".

The development of an operating model that does not address this vital question is to take a very technocratic approach to church growth and merely look at the church as an organization to which apply only organizational principles. Automatic then degenerates to, "Insert the correct amount of coins and the Coke will drop down automatically!", or, "Develop the right operating model and the church will grow automatically!"

The church must be thought of as both an organization and an organism. These two understandings must be held in tension. A superior operating model with distinctive core processes, structures, management systems and culture must be developed. At the same time, the growth principles by which God has implanted life in the church must be released, regardless of the value discipline chosen, the value proposition set forth, or the corresponding operating model developed.

I refer the reader back to chapter two and the section entitled "Building Block #1: Eight Quality Characteristics" for a detailed description of each of the quality characteristics identified by Natural Church Development. These eight quality characteristics must be built into the very core process, structure, management system, and culture of the operating model we create for the value discipline we have chosen. As we develop an operating model, how can this also be accomplished?

Learning Lessons from Nature

I had not studied Natural Church Development principles long before I came to the realization that NCD and I shared a definite theological bent and understanding. That theological bent had to do with God's creation, nature.

Christian Schwarz eloquently summarizes the position of NCD when he writes:

> Natural (or biotic) church development is an attempt to study nature, and thus God's creation, to discover principles that are applicable far beyond the realm of biology. This appeal to the biological world, the "largest and most successful organizational system we know," involves the use of analogy as a method of perception. This analogy is not concentrated on the external appearances; rather it attempts to "press on to the underlying basic principles."... "Even more productive than the study of biological structures and functions is what we can learn from the organization of biological processes, from the specific dynamics of their development and decomposition, their growth, their communication, and their self-regulation." (Paradigm, 233)

I am in full agreement with Schwarz that the biological approach is actually inherent in the scriptures (Paradigm, 234). Over and over throughout scriptures we find the biblical authors employing analogies from nature to describe the principles of God's Kingdom. This is true for both Old and New Testament writers. Did Jesus Himself use agricultural illustrations simply because he lived in an agricultural society? Would he have used illustrations from the computer world had He lived today? I think not. I concur with Schwarz' conclusion, "When the News Testament refers to organic dynamics, this is far more than metaphors that could be substituted by other imagery–rather, it speaks about real principles that operate in the world of nature as well as in the Kingdom of God. (Paradigm, 234)" Paul, following in the footsteps of Jesus, was constantly using organic illustrations. Body imagery is used everywhere (Ephesians 4:14-16; Colossians 1:18). Paul speaks constantly of fruit and fruitfulness (Galatians 5:22-23; Ephesians 5:9,11), being firmly rooted in Christ (Colossians 2:7), sowing and reaping (Galatians 6:7-8; 2 Corinthians 9:6-11; 1 Corinthians 15:42-49), first fruits (1 Corinthians 15:20-23). One would be hard pressed to contend that the saints at Ephesus, Colossae, Corinth and throughout the region of Galatia were all simply part of an agrarian society. Paul employed real principles that operate in nature and the Kingdom of God.

Borrowing Paul's illustration of the helmsman of a ship, Schwarz contends:

> Our concern in natural church development is not to try to be the *kybernetes*, the helmsman, and to develop the church with our own wisdom and strength. Our theological starting point is to allow God to be the *kybernetes*, and to let Him show us the "rules of the game." Nature teaches us what disastrous consequences it has if a technocrat plays *kybernetes*, and the same applies to the church. (Paradigm, 234)

I suggest that a starting point for developing an organic values-driven operating model is to observe the dynamics God has planted in His creation. If our God is indeed to be our *kybernetes*, we must allow Him to show us the rules of His game of life. We begin with a simple principle of scripture: "However, the spiritual is not first, but the natural; then the spiritual" (I Corinthians 15:46).

As we have noted, God's invisible things are often expressed and made manifest through His visible created order. The wisdom of preparation is seen in the life of an ant. The sluggard is to observe her ways and be wise (Proverbs 6:6-8). We are enjoined also to observe wisdom in the locust, the badger, and the lizard (Proverbs 30:24-28). We are to see stateliness in the lion, the strutting cock and the male goat (Proverbs 30:29-31). The heavens tell of God's glory. Their expanse tell of His work. Night to night reveals knowledge (Psalm 191-6). The covenant of marriage speaks to us of our relationship as the Bride to Christ our Bridegroom (Ephesians 5). Here we look to the human body, prepared uniquely by God, skillfully wrought in the depths of the earth, fearfully and wonderfully made as the work of His hands, woven in our mother's womb, made in secret (Psalm 139:13-16), to help us understand the workings of the Body of Christ.

Simple and Complex Organisms

The Single Cell -The Small Group

In the natural world, cells form the basis of all life. The cell is the most basic unit of life. The DNA contained in the nucleus of each of our cells stores enough information to build not just another cell, but also a complete human body.

In the spiritual world, the cell is the basic unit of community lived out in the world. The very life of Christ is in the cell. Christ is the DNA of cell life. The cell is where we experience the immanence of God. In the cell we experience His Presence with us, His Power through us and His Purpose for us.

The cell is where we should expect to primarily experience the manifestational giftings of the Lord. As the Spirit's giftings are manifested in cell, the Christ in you touches me, and the Christ in me touches you.

The Corporate Congregation - The Large Group

In the natural, a single-celled organism has to perform all of its life functions by itself. Cells in a multi-celled organism do not work alone. Each cell depends on the other cells to carry out their appropriate function. This interaction helps the entire organism stay alive and accomplish far more than the sum of the cells working independently. In a multi-celled organism, cells are organized into tissues, groups of similar cells that do the same sort of work. The cells in a tissue look alike. In a multi-celled organism, different tissues are further organized into organs, structures made up of differing types of tissues that work together to do a particular job. A group of organs working together to accomplish a certain function then becomes an organ system, or body system. Body systems working together comprise a complex organism.

The relationship between the individual cell and the local corporate Christian community can be likened to that relationship between a jar plunged into the Gulf of Mexico and the Gulf of Mexico itself. You submerge the jar in the Gulf of Mexico and bring it up full of Gulf of Mexico water. Everything that is in the jar is "Gulf of Mexico". Yet, not all the Gulf of Mexico is in that jar. The totality of the Gulf of Mexico cannot be contained by any one jar. In similar manner, each cell overflows as the fullness of the Body of Christ in community. Each cell is the church. Yet the totality of the church is greater than any single cell. Only as the cells are joined together do we have a body. Only as all the local expressions of Christ's Body flow together do we have the Body of Christ, the fullness of Him who fills all in all.

In the spiritual, the Body of Christ is comprised of interconnected interdependent cells, not disjointed isolated cells. Where there are no cells, only a large gathering, you have merely a massive amoebae! Where you have multitudes of cells unconnected to one another, you have merely blobs of independent protoplasm. Where you have cells vitally connected to one another and ultimately connected to the Head, Christ, then you have a Body!

Just as the manifestational giftings are the primary way in which each individual cell is built up and edified, so what will be defined as Functional Giftings are expressed for the common building up of the local corporate Body of Christ. Only in this way can we experience...

> ...the whole body, being fitted and held together by that which every joint supplies, according to the proper working of each individual part, causes the growth of the body for the building up of itself in love (Ephesians 4:16).

Christ the Head has given gifted men (Apostle, Prophet, Evangelist, Pastor, Teacher) to His corporate Body for the equipping of His saints (Ephesians 4:11). I would suggest that He has additionally created spiritual body systems working together in concert for the release into service of those thus equipped. Only as each body system works together with every other body system as the Designer created it, will the Body as a whole experience a fuller expression of the life of Christ.

Chapter 4 ☞ *Growing Stereophonic Cell Churches*

Present and Accounted for, But Undeveloped

At conception, a sperm and egg join and create that first cell. We have a human being, a baby. What we have is not potential human life! We have a human being in utero. Though that baby is but one cell, there is contained within the DNA of that cell all the necessary instructions for a full orbed life. The baby continues to grow. At birth, in a healthy and normal baby, all of the baby's bodily systems are present and accounted for. They are not all mature and fully developed, but they are all present. The child does not develop a brand new skeletal or muscular system later in life. The immune and endocrine systems do not begin in six months. The excretory system functions immediately, as does the respiratory system. They do not somehow appear later. They develop in maturity, but they are present from birth. However, in a premature birth, this may not always be the case. The baby's systems may not have developed sufficiently to sustain the baby's life. Sometimes intervention may save the baby's life. Other times the child dies.

> However, the spiritual is not first, but the natural; then the spiritual. (I Corinthians 15:46)
>
> For even as the body is one and yet has many members, and all members of the body, though they are any, are one body, so also is Christ. (I Corinthians 12:12)
>
> Now you are Christ's body, and individually members of it. (I Corinthians 12:27)

When a cell church is born, should not all the systems also be present and accounted for? They certainly could not be expected to be mature and well developed, but should they not at least be present and functioning? If the cell church is born prematurely, the cell church will likely struggle for its very life and often die because vital systems were not present or developed sufficiently to sustain life. Sometimes intervention may save its life. Other times the church will die. In transitioning situations, a similar problem exists, a problem often addressed from the top down.

Bottom Up, Not Top Down

Can these systems be decreed into existence from the "top down"? The answer is, "No!" The pitfalls here are two-fold.

First, there is the temptation on the part of a transitioning church to take the current structure of the existing church and simply impose it back upon the cells. The "hook" here is that the existing programs and activities do not have to be altered. Values and lifestyles are not thought of as having to be changed. Yet, a newborn is not ready for an adult body. The child must be allowed to grow and develop over time as the Lord directs and grants grace. That child's development may not look anything like the current church looks. Its values and lifestyle will indeed be radically different. Be advised against giving old games new names or leaping to new or altered programs without incubating values and re-ordering lifestyles!

A second temptation is for the leadership of the existing church to decree what new structures and activities will develop, seeking then to fill those new structures with members of the cells. What is the problem here? "But now God has placed the members, each one of them, in the body, just as He desired (I Corinthians 12:18)." God must place and release cell members into the body. The leadership is to function in general ways integrating the functions of all the body systems. They are to integrate and coordinate, but not decree. Looked at another way, the ministries of most churches are usually organized, developed and run from the top down. That means that the pastor, staff, board and/or elders decide to have a ministry, which is then announced to the church encouraging cell members to become a part of that ministry. It may be for a short project or a long-term commitment. That ministry, along with many other activities of the church, is then offered on a church smorgasbord from which you may fill your plate and participate.

In the cell church, ministries should not develop from the top down. Instead, they should be allowed to grow like a tree from the root upward. In a cell church, the cell is the basic Christian community. Most ministry and life takes place in the cell. Personal relationships, accountability, edification, equipping, leadership development, prayer, worship and evangelism flow out of the cell. Everyone in the Body is attached to the Body through a cell. No floating hands here! This is the first place that new believers are nurtured. As each person grows and develops, they begin to ask, "Where do I fit into the larger scheme of things? Where has God placed me in His Body? What spiritual giftings is He releasing through me? How does He want to work through my life?" Basic community will continue to keep that person plugged into the Body through the cell. Now, in addition, God is moving the person into more specific ministry in and to the larger Body of Christ.

For instance, let's look at Rich. He is faithfully functioning as a vital member in the cell. He also plays the guitar, has a heart for worship and prays, seeking to know where the Lord would have him serve. The Lord speaks to his heart to become a cell worship leader. His training, along with extra hours of ministry during the week, are now devoted to this. In this case, his sphere of ministry is still the cell. After six months of having proven ministry in this area, the corporate worship leader approaches Rich about becoming a part of an evangelistic worship team, playing guitar for one of the weekly outreaches to the city mission. Linda is ready to begin leading the worship in the cell, so Rich begins to minister on the corporate level in outreach. Jesus said that if we're faithful with a little, He'll give us more.

Note a distinctive in Dion Robert's cell church in Cote D'Ivoire, Africa. Each person is in a cell. Beyond that, each member finds what one ministry in the church they are to commit to. They do that one thing with all their heart! Imagine over 150,000 members faithfully committed to cell life and released into corporate Body ministry! Many in the states have asked the question regarding what advanced training they would receive in a cell church after they have completed the basic first year or two of equipping and as they continue in oikos evangelism. Well, what ministry has God called you to do? That's where most of your advanced training will in all likelihood be!

The life of the body is in the cell, but the body is more than a single cell. Think about it! Your body is not one big blob of protoplasm. To be sure, if you had no cells, you would have no body. However, only as each cell is joined to surrounding cells, with those cells networked into organs and in turn into body systems does your whole body become intricately united, allowing you to talk, to walk, to move, and to do a million other things that one cell alone could never do! The typical church in America tries to carry on all of its activities with 10% of the body's members doing 80% of the work. Imagine your physical body with only 20% functionality and 80% paralysis!

Now imagine a church in which every member understands their giftings, their calling, their place of ministry and they are actually released and walking it out! How many ministries could your church have if everyone were functioning properly? The potential would be almost infinite!

Remember, though, it wouldn't be because the pastor or leadership decreed we're going to have all of the ministries or form committees to get all the work done. It would have developed from the bottom up!

AN ORGANIC OPERATING MODEL - SPIRITUAL BODY SYSTEMS

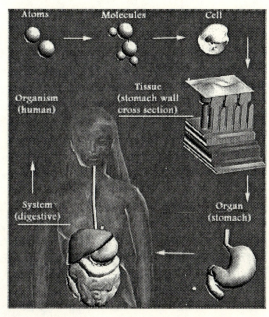

We will turn our attention now to the development of an actual organic operating model comprised of suggested spiritual body systems. These are presented neither as being comprehensive nor complete. Rather, they are presented as a new paradigm by which to understand the relationship between the gifts of the Holy Spirit and their expression in the corporate Body of Christ within a cell church. This is but step one. The second step will be the development of a comprehensive system to train and release God's people into service consistent with the call and anointing of Christ upon their life. Only then will they be able to accomplish the work of the ministry and fulfill the works God has planned from eternity past for them to walk in.

As we work through each system, keep in mind that we are to function out of our role and gifting as well as our functional ministry. We are never to shrink back from our role, be it as a servant or witness or whatever, with the excuse, "That is not my gifting!" Additionally, always remember that release into ministry in the corporate Christian community follows, not precedes, faithful service as part of the basic Christian community. Only those faithful in little will be given much.

Chapter 4 ☞ *Growing Stereophonic Cell Churches*

System #1 - The Skeletal System

Definition

The skeletal system is a mobile framework made up of 206 bones. Although individual bones are rigid, the skeleton as a whole is remarkably quite flexible and allows the human body a huge range of movement. The skeletal system is not a dead or static group of bones. Each bone is a live organ.

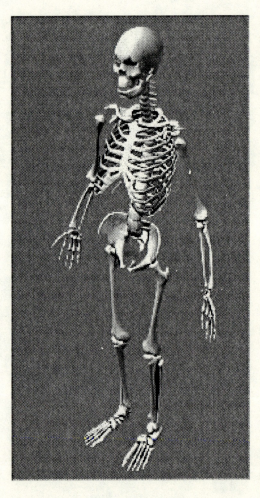

Natural Function

The skeletal system serves as an anchorage, a point of support and attachment for the skeletal muscles as well as a protective cage for the delicate internal organs of the Body. It permits flexibility of the entire body, providing a framework within which the body can express itself.

Chemical analysis resolves bone into an organic (animal) and an inorganic (earthy) material, intimately combined together. The animal matter gives to bone its elasticity and toughness, the earthy part its hardness and solidity. The proportion between these two constituents varies at different periods of life.

	Child	Adult	Old Age
Animal matter	47.20	20.18	12.2
Earthy mater	48.48	74.84	84.1

This is of practical interest to us both in the natural and by application to the Body of Christ. In the child, where the animal matter forms nearly one-half of the weight of the bone, it is not uncommon to find, after an injury happening to the bones, that they become bent, or only partially broken, due to the large amount of flexible animal matter which they contain. In older people, where the bones contain a large percent of earthy matter, the animal matter at the same time being deficient in quality and quantity, the bones are more brittle and their elasticity is destroyed. As a consequence, fracture takes place more readily. Some of the diseases to which bones are liable mainly depend upon the disproportion between the two constituents of bone.

Functional Gifting

Allow me to suggest the corresponding functional gifting within the Body of Christ is that of **Administration** (I Corinthians 12:28 Greek = Kubernao "to steer"). The one administrating acts as the "steersman" or "pilot" of a ship (Acts 27:11).

This functional gifting can be seen in operation in Acts 6:1-7 in the lives of those organizing the daily serving of food, in the parable of Jesus where the planning of resources is necessary prior to undertaking a building project (Luke 14:28-30) and in Paul's instructions to Titus to set in order what is lacking in the church on Crete (Titus 1:5).

Spiritual Function

Administration serves as an anchor for the "skeletal muscles" of the church. When correctly operative, administration permits flexibility and retards rigidity within the Body of Christ by providing a framework and structure within which the differing ministries of the Body of Christ can express themselves and through which the life and power of the Holy Spirit can be released.

Chapter 4 ☛ *Growing Stereophonic Cell Churches*

In the early life of a church, administration and structure are generally more flexible. Things are less often done strictly "by the book". The elasticity of administration and structure at this stage of life permits and even encourages continual growth of the church to occur. As a church matures in chronological age and complexity, the administration and structure generally becomes much less flexible and much more rigid. Transition and change at this point becomes very difficult, if not impossible. Does this have to happen? Not if we will guard our administration and structure from accumulating large amounts of "earthy" material that result in fossilization.

Work(s) of Service:

There are a multitude of opportunities into which "administrative" members of the Body of Christ can be released. These can include but are not limited to church administrators, financial administrators and secretarial staff. In fact, almost every ministry in the church will require administration and administrative personnel to come alongside and serve.

Those with administrative gifts can be released throughout the Body of Christ to serve in a symbiotic relationship with other members of the Body. Permit an illustration at this point. How many times are those with gifts of evangelism released by the Body to engage in mass evangelization, but find themselves bogged down with the details of planning and/or administrating the very events at which they will minister? Their energies are diffused and too often the planning is ill done. How much better to bring alongside these evangelists other members with varying degrees of giftings in administration to do that for which they are gifted anyway. Even as I write, a dear brother is preparing to preach and minister at a crusade in Haiti. His energies are divided between handling the administration involved and the preparation for public ministry.

System #2 - The Muscular System

Definition

We possess more than 600 skeletal muscles which differ in size and shape according to the jobs they do. Skeletal muscles are attached either directly or indirectly via tendons to bones. Smooth muscles, often called the in-voluntary muscles, occur in the walls of internal body organs.

Natural Function

Our muscles are our active organs of locomotion. They are formed of bundles of reddish fibers and are endowed with the property of contractility.

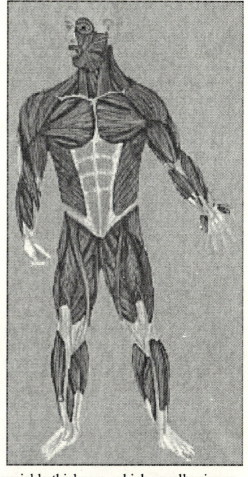

The involuntary muscular fibers form a dense interlacement, crossing each other at various angles, forming a layer of variable thickness, which usually circumscribes the wall of some cavity, which, by its contraction, it constricts.

The voluntary muscular fibers terminate at either extremity in fibrous tissue, the separate fibrillae of which in some cases form a rounded or flattened tendon. In other cases they are arranged in a more flat-

Chapter 4 ☞ *Growing Stereophonic Cell Churches*

tened manner. It is in one or other of these forms that almost every muscle is attached to the part which it is designed to move. When examining muscles, one should pay special attention to the exact origin, insertion, and actions of each, and its more important relations with surrounding parts. An accurate knowledge of their point of attachment of the muscles is of great importance in the determination of their action. By a knowledge of the action of a muscle, the surgeon is at once able to explain the causes of displacement in the various forms of fracture, or the causes which produce distortion in various forms of deformities, and consequently, to adopt appropriate treatment in each case.

Our skeletal muscles work in opposing pairs to produce the body's movements. Smooth muscles involuntarily and naturally perform such vital actions as forcing food through the intestines and pumping blood through the blood vessels. Both types of muscles provide strength and motion.

Functional Gifting

I would suggest that the corresponding functional giftings in the Body of Christ are twofold: **Service** and **Helps**.

Service (Romans 12:7) is the translation of the Greek term *diakonos*, also translated as *servant*. The functional gifting of service manifests itself through members of the Body of Christ as they identify the unmet needs involved in a task related to God's work and make use of available resources to meet those needs and help accomplish the desired goals.

This gifting is exercised "according to the proportion of one's faith". In other words, it requires faith to identify unmet needs. The attitude of one flowing in this gifting must always be that of a servant, treating others as if they were more important than themselves.

We learn from 2 Timothy 1:16-18 that Onesiphorus regularly provided hospitality for Paul when others discredited him, and also performed unspecified services for Paul at Ephesus.

helps (I Corinthians 12:28) can be defined as "a laying hold of", "to take instead of", or "take hold of".

The functional gifting of helps manifests itself through members of the Body of Christ as they invest in the life and ministry of other members of the Body, thus enabling that person helped to increase the effectiveness of his or her own spiritual gifts.

The functional gifting of helps can be illustrated out of the life and ministry of Dorcas (Acts 9:36) and Phoebe, a "helper of many" (Romans 16:1-2). Dorcas was a woman abounding with deeds of kindness and charity which she did continually. Obviously these deeds were a consistent and regular part of her life. They characterized her daily life. These deeds were done freely, from a desire to make people feel special by doing things for them which they could have done themselves but which would have seemed bothersome.

The Scriptures additionally speak of refreshing another (2 Timothy 1:16-17), serving the needs of another (Acts 6:1-7), and laying hold of and meeting another's pressing needs (Titus 3:14).

Spiritual Function

Love and servanthood allow for the mobilization of the Body of Christ. All Christians are to have the love of Christ flowing through them. All Christians are to live as servants. Yet, the Spirit especially sets some in the Body as *muscles*, designed to truly help mobilize the entire Body to perform works of service.

These *muscles* become the church's active organs of locomotion. Whether they come alongside and are involved in a task related to God's work, or whether they invest in the life and ministry of other members of the Body, releasing them into greater service, those whom God sets as *muscles* continually provide locomotion for His Body as it moves in ministry in and around the world.

As with physical muscles, those functioning as Christ's Body muscles often work in teams. Their relationships to other parts of the

Chapter 4 ☛ *Growing Stereophonic Cell Churches*

Body are especially vital. By providing strength and motion, helps and service become critical for Body health.

Work(s) of Service

Christ's *Body Muscles* perform the so-called mundane acts of service thought by many to be unspiritual, yet so necessary for the functioning of the Body of Christ in every type of ministry. They continually come alongside another to serve and help in the most practical aspects of the Christian life.

Since the gift of service includes the support of the physically weak (I Thessalonians 5:14), we need only seek to understand how the weak can be supported in order to find opportunities for service. It may mean providing transportation, purchasing groceries, performing household repairs, or providing opportunities for them to minister to others. Other activities that could express the gift of service include, but are not limited to, relief assistance or hospital/prison visitation (Matthew 25:37-40), giving physical labor (Acts 20:34-35), or assuming some of another's burdensome responsibilities (Numbers 11:16-17).

A gift of helps may be expressed as the individual comes alongside another in the Body to help them fulfill their own particular ministry. Even as a muscle aids a part of the physical body to move, the person expressing the gift of helps supports another to move forward in their God given ministry.

Two examples from my own pastoral ministry as we applied this Body paradigm may help both to illustrate the differences between service and helps and to punctuate how they move the Body of Christ.

I begin with a man whom we shall call Alain. Alain was an older retired Christian. He possessed a number of skills, one of which was woodworking, another of which was plumbing. In most of our churches Alain would not have felt a very useful or important part of the Body. However, Alain came to see himself as being a muscle in the Body with the gift of service. Alain readily would take on tasks and utilize his talents to the benefit of the Body. His release as a muscle meant the church had a platform for its sound system. His release meant the pastor and his family had an extra bathroom and two bedrooms in the basement for the older boys. His release meant the worship team could employ an actual tabernacle for its Feast of Weeks celebration. His release resulted in the actualization of the scripture "...the whole body, being fitted and held together by that which every joint supplies, according to the proper working of each individual part, causes the growth of the body for the building up of itself in love" (Ephesians 4:16).

A further example of this can be seen in the life and ministry of a woman whom we shall call Ann. Ann certainly felt like one of the more "unseemly" members of the Body. Yet, Ann exercised regularly the gift of Helps and released life into the Body. How did she accomplish this? Unlike Alain, Ann was not task oriented, but people oriented. What she did was not related to a specific task, but to helping specific people with whatever tasks they needed done. Ann had a special love for two women in the Body. The first was my secretary. Ann would come into the office regularly, most of the time unasked, to see in what ways she might help my secretary. Ann also had a special love for my wife. Ann's practical help of coming into the office one day a week to refile music and transparencies did not seem to her to be very important. However, her gift of helps was very important as her gift accomplished tasks that freed up both the Worship Leader and church secretary to concentrate on and expand their own respective ministries.

What a difference it would make if those with gifts of service and helps saw themselves as vital members of the muscular system in the Body of Christ, releasing and moving the Body into motion throughout the week, rather than as unimportant members who have little or nothing to contribute on the corporate level of Body life!

Chapter 4 ☛ *Growing Stereophonic Cell Churches*

System #3 - The Respiratory System
(Larynx; Trachea; Bronchi, Lungs)

Definition

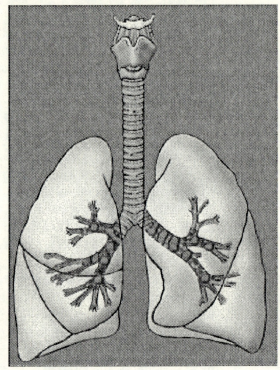

The respiratory system supplies the oxygen needed by the body's cells and then carries off their carbon dioxide waste.

Natural Function

In the natural, the respiratory system brings air into contact with the blood. The oxygen of the air can then be absorbed into the blood while the carbon dioxide, the waste product of the body, can be passed from the blood and exhaled.

Functional Gifting

I would submit to you that in the Body of Christ, those devoted to **Worship** serve such a function. The appointment of worshippers was vital throughout the scriptures (I Chronicles 16:4-7). Musicians and singers were far more than what the church of today has relegated them to — mere performers and the opening act for the pastor's message (II Chronicles 29:25).

Spiritual Function

Those who are anointed and gifted as worshippers lead the church before the throne in thanksgiving and praise, resulting in the entire Body receiving God's breath of life. Though all was prepared, it was when the trumpets and praise began that the Presence of God, His very Shekinah Glory, came mightily into His Temple, to the degree that even those ministering could no longer stand.

> ...and all the Levitical singers...with cymbals, harps, and lyres, standing east of the altar, and with the one hundred and twenty priests blowing trumpets in unison when the trumpeters and the singers were to make themselves heard with one voice to praise and glorify the Lord, and when they lifted up their voice accompanied by trumpets and cymbals and instruments of music, and when they praised the Lord saying, "He indeed is good for His loving kindness is everlasting," then the house, the house of the Lord, was filled with a cloud, so that the priests could not stand to minister because of the cloud, for the glory of the Lord filled the house. (II Chronicles 5:12-14)

Those who are anointed and appointed in the worship ministry are also those who go before the congregation and lead the church into battle (II Chronicles 20:21-22). Spiritual warfare is done most effectively in the atmosphere of worship (II Chronicles 20:21-22; Revelation 8:3-5; Acts 16:25-26).

During the large yearly gathering of the *Eglise Protestante Baptiste Oeuvres Et Mission* in Abijan, Ivory Coast, pastored by Dion Robert, when those appointed as worshippers begin to publically worship, demons begin to publically manifest. As deliverance teams busily cast out demons, worship remains an integral on-going activity. Worship brings the very breath of God into the battle. The Lord slays His enemies with the breath of His mouth (2 Thessalonians 2:8).

Work(s) of Service

Once again, the opportunities for release into worship can be nearly unlimited. Such individuals may function on worship teams for adults, youth worship teams, as worship leaders for children's ministry, providing harp and bowl worship during times of intercession,

Chapter 4 ☞ *Growing Stereophonic Cell Churches*

on dance teams, flag teams, as part of dramatic presentations, as well as leading worship at every level — Cell, Congregation and Celebration.

If worship is a basic value for a cell church, then the obvious implication is that we will worship each time we get together. These times may be cell times, corporate weekly celebration times or evangelistic events on cell, zone and corporate levels. But why limit worship to these alone? Additional times of worship ought to include seminar and training events, intercessory prayer times, leadership planning retreats, etc. In other words, those ministering in worship should be released throughout the week on every level of church life to facilitate the ushering in of the Presence of God. Your lungs are constantly in use. Pity the body where the lungs are not constantly bringing in the breath of life!

System #4 - The Urinary / Excretory System
(Kidneys; Bladder, Urethra)

Definition

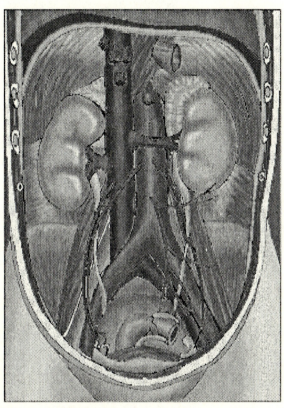

To maintain health, the body must dispose of the by-products of digestion, waste products from the repair of body tissues, medication or its breakdown process, poisonous substances, and water (to maintain the correct volume of fluid and to remove solid wastes in solution). It is the urinary / excretory system that filters waste products from the blood, by removing them from the body, often through a system of tubes.

Natural Function

The Urinary/Excretory System acts as a filtering process, removing waste products from the blood while at the same time returning certain vital chemicals and body fluids to the blood.

Functional Gifting

The giftings of **Exhortation** and **Exorcism** together make up the excretory system in the Body of Christ. Manifestations of

Exhortation and/or Exorcism are identifiable in the lives and ministry of Timothy (I Tim. 4:13-14), Paul & Barnabas (Acts 14:21-22), and Jesus in the loosing of the Daughter of Abraham Luke 13:10-16 and the corresponding granting of "the children's bread" (Mark 7:24-30).

Spiritual Function

It is those functioning in Exorcism and Exhortation that serve to reclaim and cleanse the land within each of us, land previously occupied by pockets of the enemy.

Work(s) of Service

Those in the Body of Christ flowing out of a functional gifting of **Exorcism** and/or **Exhortation** must be released to serve in areas such as soul therapy, as well as on ministry and deliverance teams.

Soul therapy and deliverance cannot be relegated to be accomplished simply on a cell level. To be sure, each cell will be involved in helping to secure the health and growth of its members, but the whole responsibility must not be left on a cell level. In the natural, each cell participates in its own cleansing, but God has so ordained the body collective that the cleansing of the entire body is the ultimate responsibility of the urinary/excretory system. In short, cleansing happens moment by moment in our cells, and moment by moment throughout our system. Such is the work of cleansing and sanctification in the Body of Christ.

Allow me another illustration to further drive this point home.It is unthinkable to give birth to a baby, take the newborn home from the hospital to a loving family, and then do nothing further to help the child grow and mature. Luke Benjamin Brickman, my grandson, was born October 16, 2001. He has received constant and continual follow-up since the moment of his birth. He is constantly watched and cared for. His every need is noticed and attended to. His growth is duly noted. Changes in his behavior are constantly observed. He is fed and changed. His parents are modeling prayer and worship and scripture reading. In short, he is not left to fend for himself.

Natural Church Development and Cell Church - Friends or Foes?

How unlike the situation in too many of our churches. A new baby is born into the Kingdom. Not wanting to intrude upon his private life, Kingdom family members give him his space and leave him on his own. He is now required to fend for himself. He has brought into this new life the uncleanness of his former existence. On top of that, he now experiences the additional soiling of this world, but is left to wash himself. No one is there to deal with deep rooted thought strongholds or practices, but many gather around to condemn him for falling short when he sins. Though a faithful cell member, he receives only remedial help and cleansing. Why? The cell is not equipped to deal with him at the level of his need. He grows with pockets of strongholds remaining for years as a Christian, struggling as the Apostle Paul notes, longing to do good, but doing it not, and feeling all the while condemned for his often secret sins.

Consider this scenario. A new child has joined the family, a son. This time it is not by birth, but by adoption. The child has come from another family who perhaps did not care for him properly, who perhaps did not demonstrate the love he needed, who perhaps born him and then left him on his own. All rejoice at the inclusion of this new family member. There is great initial excitement and enthusiasm. Yet, like with the newborn above, the excitement wanes, the enthusiasm subsides, daily regiment takes over, and the once doted over newcomer is now, like the newborn, neglected. The same fate befalls the adopted son as the natural born.

The Church has a responsibility before God to take care of those born into the Kingdom of God. Each church has a responsibility to care for those whom God places as members of a local church family.

Care and follow-up is not an option. The development of a system that will ensure quality care and follow-up is obligatory upon the church. Along with quality care and follow-up, soul therapy, accompanied by the ministry of deliverance, is fundamental to pastoral ministry and the building up of the Body of Christ. God has designed both soul therapy and deliverance as essential elements for the complete ministry program of His church. Soul therapy is what makes the church responsible and stable. It is not sufficient to simply share the gospel and lead an individual to faith in Christ. Evangelization is a process that continues. If it is truly in line with the gospel, evangelization must assure people of complete salvation. The work of soul therapy accompanied by deliverance is done with the person to finalize his level of comprehension and level of decision for Jesus.

After announcing the good news to the poor and proclaiming the year of the Lord's favor, the remainder of Isaiah 61:1-2 has practical implications for soul therapy:

> The Spirit of the Sovereign Lord is on me, because the Lord has anointed me to preach good news to the poor. He has sent me to bind up the brokenhearted, to proclaim freedom for the captives and release from darkness for the prisoners, to proclaim the year of the Lord's favor... (Isaiah 61:1-2a; Luke 4:18-19).

Jesus was sent to bind up the brokenhearted, proclaim freedom for the captives, and proclaim release to the oppressed. In other words, deal with broken hearts that need to be healed, work with those who are captive to demons or other vices, and care for those who are in anguish, depressed, sickly, oppressed by Satan, or who need to be liberated by a word of consolation and given stability. God, who initiates the work of sanctification in His people's lives can be relied upon to complete the work He has begun. A significant process He employs to bring this to pass is the work of soul therapy.

At the sunset of Jesus' life and ministry, He could state that the devil "has nothing in me" (John 14:30-31). This phraseology reflects the Hebrew אין לו עלי, commonly used in a legal sense to signify that there is no claim possible. There was nothing in the life of Jesus, no area, over which the devil could come and make claim. There were no thought patterns, no strongholds, and no actions that gave place to the enemy in His life.

Paul's closing prayer for the Thessalonians is that they would be "preserved complete, without blame" until the coming of the Lord.

He had earlier (4:3,7) emphasized the importance of sanctification and implied that it was the work of the indwelling Holy Spirit (4:8). "Spirit and soul and body" is another way of expressing his desire for their complete (ολοκληρον) sanctification. For the classical ολοκληρος (a synonym of ολοτελης) compare James 1:4, ινα ητε τελειοι και ολοκληροι, "that you may be perfect and complete" and also Acts 3:16 for the ολοκληρια, "perfect health," of the man who had been cured of his congenital lameness. Paul's desire is that every part of the Thessalonians be kept entirely without fault. That his readers be preserved entirely without fault until the Parousia, and be so found at the Parousia, at which time they will then be perfected in holiness. It is God who calls His people to sanctification (1 Peter 1:15). It is God who supplies the grace without which His call cannot be realized (faithful is He who calls you). God who initiates the work of sanctification in His people's lives can also be relied upon to complete the work.

To lead a soul to Christ is one thing, but to train, affirm, look after, and heal that soul is quite another, and is of great importance. Jesus said, "You have not chosen me but I have chosen you and ordained you, that you might go out and bear much fruit, and that your fruit should remain" (John 15:16). It is solely by the ministry of soul therapy that this will be accomplished. God gives us this command: "Know well each one of your sheep, care for your flocks" (Proverbs 27:23). Those who choose to walk with Christ come from different backgrounds (cultural, professional, and social). If the work of soul therapy is not seriously done at their particular levels, these different environments will always influence their nature (i.e. their old nature) and will hinder their spiritual faith.

The work of soul therapy and the goal of the church must be to bring each individual that has been converted to Jesus Christ to complete healing by the Holy Spirit and the Word of God. Soul therapy leads to the strengthening of the sheep. This is a corporate ministry that must go on continually.

It bears repeating, that those in the Body of Christ flowing out of a functional gifting of **Exorcism** and/or **Exhortation** must be released to serve in areas such as soul therapy and on ministry and deliverance teams within the Body. To not release them is to hinder the work of God in countless brothers and sisters through out the Body of Christ!

The Urinary / Excretory System of *Eglise Protestante Baptiste Oeuvres Et Mission*

The *Eglise Protestante Baptiste Oeuvres Et Mission* (EPBOM) in Abijan has a highly developed urinary / excretory system.

EPBOM views the fundamental work of the church and the pastor as consisting of getting close to the sheep with a view towards soul therapy. The first priority of God is to win the lost. The second priority is to take care of those who have been won. In practical terms, taking care of those who have been won entails spending time with the sheep. This means spending time with broken hearts in need of healing. This means taking whatever time is necessary with those who are captive to demons or other vices, in order to deliver them. This means coming alongside of those who are in anguish, depressed, sickly, oppressed by Satan, who need to be liberated by the word of consolation and given spiritual stability.

Because the practice of soul therapy presupposes an intimate caring relationship on the part of a pastor with one of his sheep, soul therapy then becomes the practical application of pastoral love and concern. For that to happen there must be trust between the one applying soul therapy and the one to whom it is applied. Soul therapy will only work if the one applying it knows the one to whom it is being applied and is full of love for them. Pastor Dion is clear on the distinction between merely being acquainted with the sheep and knowing the sheep:

> You must take care of their problems. It is in this way, through soul therapy, that love is applied. You must love them to set them free. You must love them to work with their problems, which are very deep, and heal the brokenhearted, free them

> from the powers of darkness and share with them what we have. The life of sharing - sharing their sufferings, that is where soul therapy is necessary. That is where the sharing of life is necessary (Dion, Interview).

The ministries of soul therapy and deliverance are under the authority of the Department of Demonology. Pastor Wouehi Louan Etienne oversees that department. Pastor Etienne likens soul therapy to a surgical operation performed in the life of a new believer:

> After he says, "Hey, what can I do to be saved?" that is when we do soul therapy. That is where we do surgery. In surgery, in an operation, that is where it hurts. You like smoking. You like it a lot. You didn't think you could ever separate from it. It is as if we have operated on you. Against your own desires, but because of Jesus, you'll abandon it. "Oh, pastor it is not easy!" "Take courage. Three days. It will work." Little by little he abandons it. He is a thief and he steals. When he steals he then dresses well. In soul therapy we discover that he steals. We tell him, "Stop stealing. God doesn't like it. The thief will not go to heaven." We will read the Bible about what God says about the thief. "If you continue to steal you will not be in agreement with God. If you continue to steal, you will be troubled." He says, "Oh, really. So I need to stop stealing and abandon it." Now Satan at the same time says, "How are you going to dress now?" So, it becomes a fight. Soul therapy is fighting, fighting in the spiritual war. Satan says to steal, but he won't steal. "Steal!" "I won't steal!" It is a fight. That is soul therapy. (Interview)

Soul therapy presupposes a spiritual battle. A sheep fighting against the adversary is desperately seeking and needing support, security and direction from his leaders. "To render the soul of a sheep clean we must come against 3 forces: strongholds, reasoning and arrogance" (Robert, Soul Therapy 46). In the lives of God's people there are often strongholds that need to be torn down. They may be demonic hereditary ties. They may involve some form of demonization by evil spirits. Through soul therapy these strongholds can be torn down and the man or woman of God freed from bondage and enslavement by the powers of darkness.

In their ministry of soul therapy and deliverance, those involved make a clear distinction between what might be called "fruits" and "roots", that is, presenting symptoms and underlying causes.

Three threads continually run through EPBOM's ministry of soul therapy: obedience, submission, and humility. For soul therapy to be effective, the person must embrace obedience. Remember that the goal of soul therapy is to bring the child of God to a life of humility under the mighty hand of God. The intent is to accomplish total submission to the word of God in place of religious and philosophical practices that lead them astray.

The effectiveness of this body system at EPBOM is evidenced by its fruit, both qualitatively and quantitatively. For a fuller description of this body system and its fruit, and how this system is interrelated with the other systems at EPBOM, I refer the reader to my earlier work, *Preparing the 21st Century Church*.

System #5 - The Digestive System
(Stomach; Small & Large Intestine; Spleen)

Definition

The digestive system receives, digests and absorbs food. Digestion is the chemical process by which the proteins, fats and carbohydrates of food are broken down into smaller chemical units which are then capable of being absorbed into the body.

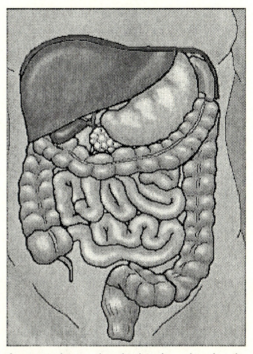

Natural Function

In the body, digestion is a chemical process that takes complex food substances and reduces them to components the body can process. It is thus the process of taking the complex and reducing it to its simple elements for processing by others.

Functional Gifting

The gift of **Teaching** is one of the more obvious functional giftings seen in scripture. Scriptures are replete with illustrations. We need only examine the ministry of Apollos (Acts 18:24-28), Paul (Acts 20:20-21), the elders of Ephesus (Acts 20:28) and the mention of teachers in I Corinthians 12:28-29 and Ephesians 4:11-14.

Spiritual Function

Those set in this function within the Body of Christ teach and feed the flock of God by taking the sometimes complex things of God and breaking them into elements the rest of the Body can absorb.

Work(s) of Service

Those recognized as teachers should be released to teach the corporate Body, specific sub-groupings within the corporate Body such as children, youth, single adults, men, women, etc., and various other groupings as needed at varying levels (sub-zone; zone; district; congregation), at varying times and varying locations (seminars and retreats).

We have correctly proclaimed that the cell is not to serve as a Bible study, but the basic Christian community. many cell churches no longer have an adult Sunday School. The Body of Christ, however, is still in need of systematic teaching. Theological truths must be somehow broken down into bite size morsels for consumption by the average Christian. If not, then the too oft heard charge against cell churches of biblical ignorance on the part of its members will unfortunately become true.

Theological teaching cannot be done solely vis-a-vis the pastor's message during a Sunday corporate gathering. Neither can it be accomplished in the cell meeting. Neither will it be accomplished by Christians left on their own to read whatever books they may fancy.

God has set teachers in His Body to teach the body. They are the Body of Christ's digestive system. Without their functioning, the body will become anemic and eventually will starve to death. We are anemic today. If we do not change the course we are on, our anemia will turn to death tomorrow.

System #6 - The Circulatory System
(Heart; Arteries; Capillaries; Veins)

Definition

The circulatory system provides all body tissues with a regular supply of oxygen and nutrients and carries away carbon dioxide as well as other waste products.

Natural Function

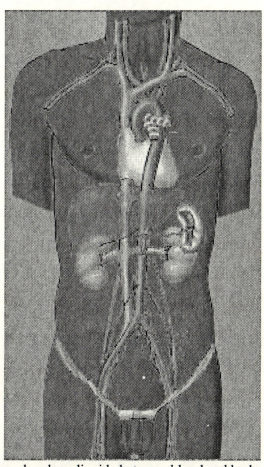

The blood which carries nutriment and oxygen to all the tissues of the body and carries waste products away from the tissues is pumped through a closed system of tubes known as the circulatory system. This system allows for the care and the nurture of each cell of the body. Capillaries allow for the exchange of oxygen and carbon dioxide between blood and body cells. On its journey from the heart to the tissues, blood is forced along the arteries at high pressure. However, on the return journey through the veins and back to the heart, the blood is at low pressure. It is kept moving by the muscles in the arms and legs compressing the walls of the veins, and by valves in the veins preventing the blood from flowing backward. The interdependence of the muscular system and the circulatory system should be duly noted.

Functional Gifting

Mercy and **Giving** function as the circulatory system within the Body of Christ. The churches of Macedonia themselves functioned as part of the larger Body of Christ's circulatory system, circulating the wealth and provision of God to those churches in need (II Corinthians 8:1-7). In a local setting, widows benefited from this ministry in Acts 6:1.

Spiritual Function

By means of mercy and giving there results care and nurture of all the members of the Body of Christ.

While it is true that all are called to live giving lives and walk in mercy to those around them, there will be those within the corporate Christian community that especially evidence the giftings of mercy and giving. They will often be those catalysts and conduits whom God has established to bring and transmit compassion.

Within the larger corporate Body, these will remind the people of God that they are to be more than the army of God, they are also to be the family of God, evidencing the compassion of the Father toward those without and within.

Work(s) of Service

Specific acts of mercy and giving can be performed for the sick, widows, orphans, and the handicapped, to name but a few. Especially allow those whom God sets in the Corporate Christian Community with gifts of mercy and giving to challenge the community not only to minister to those in need within the Body, but to also together engage in acts of servant evangelism, preparing the way for the gospel of peace for those outside the Body (Ephesians 6:15).

System #7 - The Endocrine System
(Pituitary; Adrenal; Thyroid)

Definition

The endocrine system is one of two systems providing overall control over other body functions and in general integrating the functions of all the body systems.

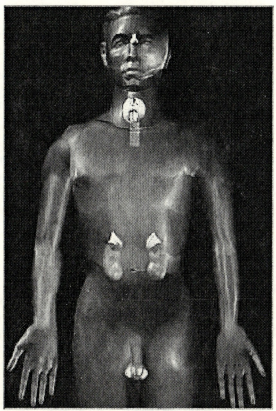

Natural Function

The endocrine system produces hormones which act to regulate, integrate and coordinate a wide variety of chemical processes carried on by the other tissues and organs of the body. The adrenal cortex maintains blood pressure and the body's salt balance. The thyroid produces the hormones necessary to stimulate metabolism, body heat production and bone growth. The parathyroid maintains the calcium level in the blood. The Endocrine system provides for vital balance throughout the body.

Some common endocrine disorders include Addison's disease and Cushing's syndrome. People with Cushing's syndrome develop thin skin that bruises easily. The bones become weakened and are at risk of fracturing. Mental changes often occur, including depression, paranoia, or sometimes euphoria. Insomnia may be a problem. In children, Cushing's syndrome may suppress growth.

Functional Gifting

The endocrine system correlates with the functional gifting of **Leading**. Paul writes of elders who rule well (I Tim. 5:17) and indeed, the Council at Jerusalem was comprised of those set in the Body with this function (Acts 15:1-35). God grants such gifted men and women as leaders to the trans-local Church (Ephesians 4:11) as well as to each local church (Hebrews 13:17).

Spiritual Function

It is those set as leaders who establish purpose and vision for the overall Body. They are the ones who define an overall philosophy of ministry. Having spent intimate time alone with God, it is the leader(s) who articulates the church's value system, establishes her priorities, determines her practices, and oversees the working of her programs and personnel.

It is interesting to note some of the "diseases" that also affect Christ's endocrine system (leadership). How many leaders have we known over the years that are afflicted with **Cushing's Syndrome**? You know the disease well and have probably encountered it often. When afflicted, the pastor and/or leaders wear their feelings on their shoulders and their thin skin bruises very easily. We hear various comments about such leaders. "Man, is he really touchy!" "We have to treat that elder with kid gloves." Leadership at every level must guard against contracting Cushing's Syndrome with the accompanying development of thin skin and a tendency to bruise easily. Those that lead must constantly guard against being "touchy" or "overly sensitive" as they lead, lest the growth and development of the Body be hindered and suppressed. I remember well one pastor around whom everyone tiptoed, lest they offend him. You dared not tell him the truth, and had to phrase your sentences in such a way that they would not give the wrong impression and offend him. You never knew what kind of mood he would be in.

Addison's disease is another common ailment that throws the Body of Christ out of vital balance. Like Cushing's Syndrome, leaders need to guard against contracting Addison's disease and the accompanying development of moodiness or mental depression and paranoia characteristic of its presence. I knew of one prominent church that suffered long with the pastor's depressive moods. A pall hung over the church. I visited another church a number of years back in which the pastor publicly apologized during the Sunday evening service for 18 months of depression that he acknowledged had sapped the very life out of his people. Talk about paranoia, some leaders are sure their boards or elders or people are "out to get me". They are constantly tormented with the worry that the whispering they think they hear is about them!

When the endocrine system is working improperly, the whole Body suffers. This is not to say leaders may not experience problems, but they must be healed for the health of the Body.

Work(s) of Service

These leaders may serve as elders, as part of the pastoral ministry team, as well as leaders at more basic levels of ministry. Such individuals may be called such things as a Senior Pastor, Staff, Zone Pastor, etc.

System #8 - The Nervous System
(Brain; Sense Organs - Smell, Sight, Hearing, Taste, Touch)

Definition

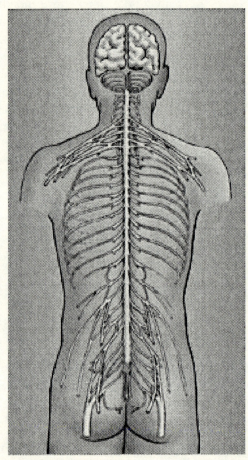

The nervous system is a vast network of connected cells which comprise: 1) the brain (our most complex and least understood organ), 2) the spinal cord, and 3) the peripheral nerves. The nervous system can "sense changes," both in the body and in the outside environment. The nervous system also integrates information and controls body movement and internal body functions. In order to sustain life, the nervous system must maintain a state of homeostasis (that is, balance or equilibrium) in response to changes of the outside world. The nervous system is the second of two systems providing overall control over other body functions and integrating the functions of the body systems in general.

Natural Function

The nervous system allows the body to react to its external environment. It enables and coordinates sensory input. It can be best thought of as the electrical wiring and control panel of the human body. The nerves are the wires which carry electrical signals from the sensory organs (receptors) to the main trunk line (spinal cord) to a central control panel and switchboard called the brain.

The nervous system is divided anatomically between: 1) the central nervous system (CNS), which includes the brain and spinal cord, and 2) the peripheral nervous system (PNS). The PNS includes the cranial nerves, that are connected to the brain and the spinal nerves, joined to the spinal cord.

The nervous system may also be divided according to function. The somatic nervous system and the autonomic nervous system are two functional classifications of the nervous system. The somatic nervous system is involved in conscious perception of the environment and voluntary movement of the body. The autonomic nervous system senses the body's internal environment and controls involuntary functions such as heart rate, gastrointestinal contractions, and glandular secretions.

A sub-system of the autonomic nervous system increases the body's available energy, and is active when a person is under stress. It is named the fight or flight system. Another sub-system, on the contrary, increases the storage of energy and controls normal resting activities such as the digestion of food. This is sometimes referred to as the rest and repair system.

Functional Gifting

The nervous system correlates with the functional gifting of **Prophecy**. Before we begin to explore this part of the Body of Christ, we must note from the outset the distinctions between prophetic manifestations, prophetic ministry, and those that occupy the prophetic office.

Paul mentions prophetic manifestations in I Corinthians 12:10. Let it be affirmed that while not all believers are prophets (I Corinthians 12:29), all may from time to time manifest prophesy (I Corinthians 14:31,39). Such prophetic manifestations should be judged as to whether they give exhortation, encouragement, strengthening, edification or consolation (I Corinthians 14:3, 24-25; Acts 15:32).

Paul speaks of prophetic ministry in Romans 12:6. Examples of those flowing in prophetic ministry include Judas and Silas (Acts 15:30-33) and the daughters of Philip (Acts 21:9-11). Although it appears the scriptures refer to his daughters as prophetesses, the Greek text refers to them as those who are simply prophesying (verb), not as prophetesses (noun). Many in the Body of Christ will be ministering prophetically. We do them and the Lord a disservice by calling "prophets" those that simply flow in prophetic ministry. As seen in Acts 13, there were those in the church recognized as holding the Prophetic office. This is different from merely manifesting prophetic giftings or even exercising prophetic ministry.

Anyone in the Body of Christ may manifest the gifting of prophecy (1 Corinthians 12:10) to meet a specific need. In that sense, all may prophesy (1 Corinthians 14:31). Some in the Body may exercise this gifting on a regular basis for the edification of the whole Body. They will grow in this prophetic ministry (Acts 21:9-11). However, Prophets are one of those 5-Fold Ministry Gifted Servants the ascended Lord has given to His Body for the equipping of the saints for the work of service to the building up of the Body of Christ. They occupy the Prophetic office in the church.

Spiritual Function

Just as the nervous system can "sense changes" both in the physical body and in the outside environment, so the prophetic ministry, through their prophetic awareness and sensitivity, can sense changes both in the Body of Christ and the natural/supernatural world around them.

The prophetic ministry enables and coordinates sensory input that then allows the Body of Christ to correctly respond to the ever changing surrounding environment. In response to these changes, the prophetic ministry helps the Body of Christ maintain balance and equilibrium. Thus, like the nervous system, the prophetic ministry is

Natural Church Development and Cell Church - Friends or Foes?

involved in conscious perception of the outside environment and voluntary movement of the Body in response. This can be seen in Acts 15:30-33. The church in Antioch had been disturbed by false doctrine. The result was the agitation and unsettling of the church. Judas and Silas carried a letter from Jerusalem designed to correct the situation. Even though the letter brought rejoicing and encouragement to the church, Judas and Silas, being themselves prophets, further encouraged and strengthened the brethren with a lengthy message, thereby providing for the church additional balance and equilibrium.

In response to internal changes, the prophetic ministry, like the autonomic nervous system, senses the body's internal environment and triggers the functions of other body systems in response. When the body is placed under stress, the nervous system will prepare the body to either fight or flee through the release of additional adrenaline.

In like manner, when the Body of Christ is under stress, the prophetic ministry increases the Body's available energy, preparing the Body for a fight or flight. Paul was in this way prepared through the prophetic ministry of Agabus as recorded in Acts 21:11. It is interesting to note that the response of the others present was for Paul to flee. Paul, however, was prepared to advance forward into the fight.

At other times, the prophetic ministry acts as a rest and repair system, increasing the storage of energy in the Body of Christ. When released during times of corporate gathering, the prophetic ministry will bring rest and repair to the Body of Christ while increasing the present level of energy as they minister edification (building up) and exhortation and consolation (I Corinthians 14:3-4).

Work(s) of Service

Works of service will include prophetic ministry operating at all levels, personal, cell, congregation and celebration.

I have observed over the years great internal conflict between the pastoral ministry of a church and the prophetic ministry. Rather than work in harmony, as do the endocrine and nervous systems, they live in opposition to one another. Allow me to suggest a number of reasons for this condition, and how to bring balance back to Christ's Body.

Many pastors and senior elders placed by God in the endocrine system to provide oversight and leadership are intimidated by the prophetic ministry. Often their attitude is, "If God really wanted to speak that kind of a word, He can speak directly to me as the pastor." At times this attitude is a result of their own insecurity. Often such an attitude is a reaction against what has been brought by the prophetic, or more frequently, how it has been brought. It is rare for a Senior elder to say about the prophetic, "I need you!"

There must be an acceptance and receiving of the prophetic by the pastoral. God has set each one in the Body as it pleased Him. One system cannot say to another, "I have no need of you." Each system is vital. The pastoral must understand that they do not have to get every word of the Lord that comes. They do not have to see every vision, dream every dream, receive every prophetic revelation. Their responsibility is to judge, interpret and apply what the prophetic has spoken forth. It is the responsibility of the prophetic to sense what is happening outside the Body, warn, prepare the Body for action, help bring about an inner state of homeostasis. The pastoral is set in the Body to regulate, coordinate, and integrate the functions of the rest of the Body, not to usurp those functions.

Often the prophetic, because of what they sense, place pressure on the pastoral to "Do something!" Often the prophetic feels like it also knows what should be done. Herein lies their error. Allow me to suggest that those with prophetic giftings will receive revelation from the Lord. They then do have a responsibility to speak that which they see or sense to the pastoral. But here their responsibility ends. The interpretation of that which they have seen, and then the application of that which they have seen or heard is not their responsibility before God. They are simply to give forth the message and trust the endocrine system to make appropriate changes and responses in the body collective.

Natural Church Development and Cell Church - Friends or Foes?

This weekend I had a call from a former member who had received a prophetic word for me. This individual I have known well for over thirteen years. They have a most humble and teachable spirit. They are willing receive instruction and when necessary, correction. Their words for me have to date all been correct. They had recently come under intense pressure as they were receiving a number of words for people who they did not know, and had been told they must interpret their words and apply them to the person's life also. What an unnecessary burden they had been placed under. They experienced great liberation when they again realized that their responsibility was to deliver the word, not interpret and apply it for another.

In my own church experience, when we learned to receive one another and the place God has placed each one in His Body, the endocrine and nervous systems dwelt together in peace. Truly, how good and pleasant it is for brothers to dwell together in unity!

Chapter 4 — *Growing Stereophonic Cell Churches*

System #9 - The Reproductive System

Definition
Reproductive organs located in the pelvis.

Natural Function
When the body comes of age, the reproductive system enables procreation and the carrying on of life.

Functional Gifting:
The corresponding functional gifting in the Body of Christ is that of **Evangelism & Missionary**. This can again be illustrated from the life of Philip who served first as a deacon (servant) and ultimately as an evangelist (Acts 8:4-8; 8:26-40; 21:8). Paul also was sent to evangelize the Gentiles (Acts 22:21) and to church plant (Acts 13:1-3). Timothy also was called to do the work of an evangelist (II Timothy 4:5). Some are specifically called and given to the Body of Christ (Ephesians 4:11-14) to bring glad tidings (Romans 10:15) and at times function with a city wide ministry (Acts 14:21). They have a stew-

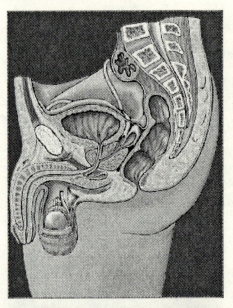

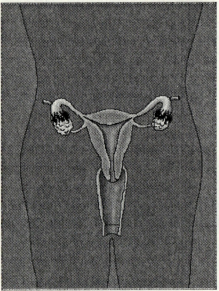

ardship entrusted to them (I Corinthians 9:16-18). Again, note the difference between all of us having the responsibility to be a witness, while others are released with a functional gifting of evangelism, while still others are called and released in the Body as Evangelists.

Spiritual Function
Reproduction of the life of Christ in others.

Work(s) of Service
Works of service may include but not be limited to church planting, missionary work and mass evangelization.

Chapter 4 ☞ *Growing Stereophonic Cell Churches*

System #10 - The Immune System

Definition:

The Immune System protects the body from disease, making the body resistant to particular diseases.

Natural Function:

The human body has many ways to protect itself. Some are simply physical barriers, like the skin's tough outer layer that shields living cells beneath it from a hostile environment. Others are potent biochemical substances that offer relatively non-specific protection against a broad range of microorganisms. For example, tears contain an enzyme which acts to digest and weaken the protective walls surrounding bacterial cells.

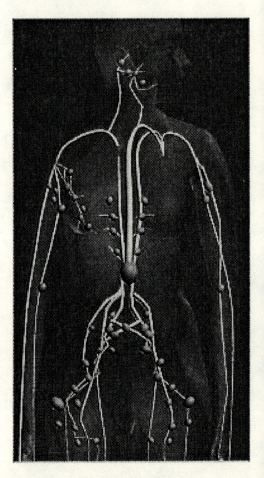

But by far the most complex, dynamic and effective strategies are carried out by specialized cells that travel through the body to search out and destroy microorganisms and other foreign substances. In human beings, three major groups of cells provide this type of defense. Two of these specialized cells act primarily by engulfing and digesting bacteria, cellular debris, and other particulate matter. Following engulfment, a metabolic burst occurs and the engulfed matter is then gradually but relentlessly broken down. Ultimately, the offending particles are usually annihilated. Some materials may resist degradation but still remain sequestered within the cells and so are prevented from contacting the surrounding tissue. For example, large numbers of inhaled carbon particles often persist for years in the lungs of cigarette smokers, encased within these cells. The third group, which in part comprise our lymph system, participates in a host of protective reactions that are known as immune responses. In effect, they detect foreign invasion and alert the body to begin carrying out specific defensive measures against the foreign invader.

Both classes of cells are essential for health. They often act in concert and are to a great extent dependent on one another for maximal effectiveness. Thus, we observe in the natural that the immune system lessons liability on the part of the body to injury through foreign invasion.

Functional Gifting

Like the lymph system, it is the intercessors that often are the first to detect foreign invasion and alert the rest of the Body to carry out specific defensive measures. Often, a group of intercessors will engulf offending invaders, gradually but relentlessly breaking them down until they are annihilated from the Body. Through their constant intercessory prayers, the enemy is often prohibited from ever contacting the rest of the Body.

Such is the ministry and function of intercession. Though all are to gather and pray (Acts 12:12), some are called and gifted and function within the Body of Christ as intercessors. Both Epaphras and Paul, as they prayed on behalf of the Colossian church, give evidence to this spirit of intercession (Colossians 4:12; 1:9-12). We see intercession for the nations and those in authority (I Tim. 2:1-2), for the Church as a whole (Col 1:9-12), for the local Body of believers (Colossians 4:12-13), for those in trouble (ex: Peter Acts 12:12), the demonized (Mark 9:14-29, especially verse 29), for the sick (James 5:14-16) and for the lost (Romans 10:1).

Two members of my own family have had lymphatic cancer. You can imagine the seriousness of this form of cancer. Not only is there a disease of rebellious cells attacking the physical body, but, worse yet, the cancer has even infiltrated the very system designed to resist it. In so doing, the cancer has both disabled the body's defense mechanism and has turned that very system against the body itself, as it uses the lymphatic system to spread its rebellion throughout the rest of the body.

Employing the same strategy, the enemy of the Body of Christ seeks to cripple the ministry of intercession and open the Body up to every form of spiritual attack and malignancy while our defense shields are down. Remember similar scenes from Star Wars? Satan would also seek to plant a cancer of gossip or criticism or division into the gathering of intercessors, resulting in the spread of death, rather than life and health throughout the Body!

Spiritual Function

Spiritually, intercession is our defense system capable of incapacitating the enemy and his designs against us.

Work(s) of Service

Intercession may be released during ministry times, before, during and after services, as well as during the week on behalf of the Body of Christ and the nations.

Like the prophetic, there is often a conflict between the intercessory prayer ministry and the pastoral ministry within a church. You most likely have heard the horror stories of how a seemingly innocent group of "prayer warriors" began to manipulate the pastor through what they "received" from the Lord while in prayer. Great havoc has been wrought in many American Charismatic churches by "intercessory prayer groups". How can it be avoided without throwing out the proverbial baby with the bath water?

Like the prophetic ministry, the intercessory prayer ministry must recognize they can pray and intercede, but then they must leave with the pastoral ministry that which they have received. Their words and visions must be judged, interpretation made, and correct application applied. This is not their responsibility to do, nor even to influence those whose responsibility it is. They must lay it at the leaders' feet, receive the endocrine system's judgment, and rest in the application to follow. In other words, the immune system must subordinate itself to that integrating and coordinating system, the endocrine system. When it fails to do so, it finds itself fighting the very Body it is placed to protect and becomes destructive to the Body, similar to an auto-immune disease like AIDS. When it does submit, the Body is assured of a strong and healthy immunological system fighting off the attacks of the enemy.

IMPLICATIONS

Task Groups

As we close this chapter, revisit with me a moment the thinking today of many American "cell church" pastors. Their underlying contention is that, "Cells will not work here like they do elsewhere throughout the world!" As a consequence, many then decide to develop task groups. How utterly superfluous are task groups in the paradigm just presented! The development of task groups is totally anachronistic within the context of church members living in constant community, receiving training for the deployment of their spiritual gifts, being mobilized into a corporate Body whose very structure is considered to be the manifestation of the gift of God and where there exists balance between cell life and corporate life. What can task groups possibly accomplish that cannot be accomplished more effectively and more efficiently on a corporate level through a totally mobilized body of believers? Task groups can add nothing! To have task groups is a throwback to a bygone era when the church was undeveloped and unable to perform the work of the Kingdom.

I would unequivocally contend that the development of task groups on the scale currently being witnessed today in America and the parading of task groups as somehow being "cells" is, by its very nature, a sharp rebuke to the American cell church movement and an indication of our own immaturi-

Chapter 4 ☞ *Growing Stereophonic Cell Churches*

ty and failure to correctly develop the large group wing and the small group wing of what Bill Beckham has called the two-winged church. Until we restore that balance, this bird will never be able to soar in the heavens, fulfilling once more the bidding of the Master!

Cells and community go hand in glove. Out of the cell edification, equipping, evangelism and empowering comes the identification and release into corporate ministry of each member according to their spiritual giftings. As a consequence, every individual is living in community (cell wing) as well as functioning out of their gifts as a part of the larger Body (corporate wing). What ministry of the church can a single cell accomplish that cannot be better accomplished by the release of the life resident within the corporate body? None!

A Biblical Model

The biblical model of the church is that of an organization and organism, a body which must operate with every part in dependency upon every other part. Organically, the Body of Christ is comprised of interconnected interdependent cells, not disjointed isolated cells. Where there are no cells, only a large gathering, you have merely a massive amoebae! Where you have multitudes of cells unconnected to one another, you have merely blobs of independent protoplasm. Where you have cells vitally connected to one another and ultimately connected to the Head, Christ, then you have a Body! Christ has one Body in unity with many members in diversity. All the members have been appointed by God, placed by God in the Body as He desired. All have differing gifts. All possess differing functionality in any local setting. Only as each member functions correctly will the Body corporately function correctly.

In an organism, placement requires calling and giftedness. People are raised up at the initiation of the Spirit. The Body confirms and releases what God is at work doing. Christ the Head has given gifted men (Apostle, Prophet, Evangelist, Pastor, Teacher) to His corporate Body for the equipping of His saints (Ephesians 4:11). He has additionally created body systems working together in concert for the release into service of those thus equipped. Only as each body system works together with every other body system as the Designer created it, will the Body as a whole experience the fuller expression of the life of Christ.

Body Systems and Biotic Principles

The body systems are **interdependent**. No system is complete in and of itself. No system is an island. The decisions made regarding one body system will impact, for good or ill, all the other systems. when those in one system suffer, the entire body suffers. When those in one system are honored, all are honored. One cannot merely focus on one system doing its work independent of another. The systems must move together as one.

Built into each system is the principle of **multiplication**. For sustainable healthy growth of the whole body, the church, each system must reproduce and multiply itself at all levels. Thus, reproduction is part of the job description of each Christian set within each system. To merely utilize their own giftings in ministry is insufficient. They must reproduce themselves and empower others in ministry. As the quality characteristic of empowering leadership is enhanced, the overall level of health of the body will be increased.

Christian Schwarz notes three effects of releasing gift-oriented ministry in the church. "When Christians serve in their area of giftedness, they generally function less in their own strength and more in the power of the Holy Spirit. Thus ordinary people can accomplish the extraordinary! (NCD, 24). Third the research discovered that "no factor influences the contentedness of Christians more than whether they are utilizing their gifts or not. (NCD, 24)" Therefore, as individuals minister out of their giftedness, positive **energy** will be released and can be channeled, while negative energy will be minimized as Christians become more content in their personal life.

Once the body systems have been developed, they will soon become self-sustaining as members not only themselves do the work of the ministry, but continually raise up others, especially those new believers who have benefited from their ministry. Those set free through the work of the excretory system can be encouraged to become part of that system. Some of the energy expended each week by the respiratory system should also be directed toward raising up additional leaders in that system. Those that are faithful in little may be given more. **Energy spent will be re-invested** to make the system increasing self-sustaining.

The physiological systems of the human body live in mutual **symbiosis**. Each system actively cooperates with all the rest. There is linkage between the circulatory system which transports oxygen and each of the other systems that desperately need that oxygen for life. If not for the excretory system, than waste produced by the digestive system would kill the body. The systems of the body do not compete for resources. When one or more systems compete rather than cooperate, we say the body has cancer, or an auto-immune deficiency. So also the Body of Christ. When God is allowed to place each one in the appropriate system as He desires, there will be a state of homeostasis. God has so composed the body that there should be no division (1 Corinthians 12:25).

As systems come on line, so to speak, there will be no confusion as to their specific **function**. Those within each system will minister with a clear sense of purpose. They will understand where they fit into God's greater creation and bear the appropriate fruit. They will experience a sense of fulfilling their destiny.

Each body system and its corresponding gifting has been briefly examined. Once this paradigm is embraced, basic changes must be made that will allow a developing cell church to live as an organism. Giving old games new names or leaping to new programs without incubating values will not do. There must be the development of a comprehensive system to train and release God's people into service consistent with the call and anointing of Christ upon their life. To avoid frustrating those desiring to be released into body ministry and service to God, a thorough system must be established for the identification, training and release of the various body members into their God called and gifted ministries of service. Only then will they be able to accomplish the work of the ministry and fulfill the works God has planned from eternity past for them to walk in.

5

Learning to Think and Plan Biotically

Transitioning Small Groups to Cells

Then the Lord answered me and said, "Record the vision and inscribe it on tablets, that the one who reads it may run. For the vision is yet for the appointed time; it hastens toward the goal and it will not fail. Though it tarries, wait for it; For it will certainly come, it will not delay.

Habukkak 2:2-3

Chapter 5 ☛ *Learning to Think and Plan Biotically*

TRANSITIONING CURRENT SMALL GROUPS TO CELLS

A Common Issue

In the mid 1990's it was generally only the innovators and early adopters who embarked upon a transition of their small groups to cell groups in America. As cells have demonstrated some degrees of "success" over the years, more and more pastors, the early and late majority, are considering making the move from a traditional small group approach to a cell paradigm in their church. During this same period of time, Natural Church Development has also demonstrated its values and benefits to the American church scene. More and more churches are utilizing the NCD survey and availing themselves of NCD coaching support. As an ever increasing number of churches embrace the cell church paradigm, can the principles of Natural Church Development actually help in their transition from "small groups" to "cell groups?"

Can Natural Church Development Help? - Biotic Decision Making

Applying Natural Church Development in the context of growing a cell church means more than simply making decisions that will improve the church's minimum factor. It means making biotic decisions whenever decisions are made by the leadership team. Biotic decisions are just what the name implies, decisions that have been fundamentally thought through and filtered through the six biotic principles. The basic assumption is that where decisions have not employed a biotic filter, "all by itself growth" will be less likely to occur than where a biotic filter has been employed.

A church has limited resources. To waste resources carrying out decisions that do not contribute to "all by itself" growth is poor stewardship. The most effective use of a church's resources occurs when the resources are allocated based upon biotic decision making. I would define a church's resources in terms of its time, energy, and material. Decisions should not be made before the cost has been clearly counted. As Bill Beckham is fond of quoting, "Where the vision is unclear, the cost is always too high." We must have clear vision of the cost before we allocate our limited resources. In Luke 14:28-32 Jesus puts it this way:

> For which one of you, when he wants to build a tower, does not first sit down and calculate the cost to see if he has enough to complete it? Otherwise, when he has laid a foundation and is not able to finish, all who observe it begin to ridicule him, saying, 'This man began to build and was not able to finish.' Or what king, when he sets out to meet another king in battle, will not first sit down and consider whether he is strong enough with ten thousand men to encounter the one coming against him with twenty thousand? Or else, while the other is still far away, he sends a delegation and asks for terms of peace.

The biotic principles help clarify our vision before making a decision. They assist the leadership in looking at the church as an organism and in a holistic, integrative way, before making decisions. **Interdependence** reminds us that whatever we do to one part of the organism will effect all its other parts. **Multiplication** will require us to consider how whatever we initiate will produce results which multiply. **Energy transformation** will force us to examine all the energy in the church and consider how to harness the untapped energy, while at the same time directing the positive energies and redirecting the negative energies already present. **Multi-usage** warns us against investing initial time, energy and material, only to have to constantly repeat the process. Our goal should be for whatever we initiate to grow to the point where it begins operating on its own. **Symbiosis** helps us remember to promote cooperation rather than competition within the church as a whole. **Functionality** helps ensure we reach our destination and bear fruit for the Kingdom of God by forcing us to clearly define our purpose.

By encouraging biotic decision making, I am not implying that leadership decisions in the average cell church never employ any of these grids. To some extent they can be observed operating in every church, whether as a result of leadership intuition, secular training, or simply God's grace. What is at issue is proactivity. I am suggesting we proactively give these principles high priority and specific attention when making decisions that then result in the allocation of our church's resources.

The bottom line is this. As we learn to make better and better decisions using the biotic principles, blockages to growth will be anticipated and removed, our resources will be more effectively allocated, and we will be actively cooperating with God to maximize our church's potential for "all by itself" healthy growth.

Let's examine a typical church, Riverside Community Church (RCC) in Nutley, New Jersey. The Senior Pastor, Don Flynn, and the leadership team both desire to transition their current small groups, which they have called Growth Groups, to cell groups. Let's look at the church's background, present challenges, and a suggested scenario for initial transition. We will then attempt to apply the biotic principles to the transition scenario suggested by Riverside's leadership team as they seek to transition from Growth Groups to cell groups.

CASE STUDY -
RIVERSIDE COMMUNITY CHURCH!

Background

Riverside's government is a cross between congregational and presbyterian, more towards the latter. Decisions are made by the board, and board members are elected by the membership. In practice, the way it works is that the board is the decision making body. The Senior Pastor chairs the board and has a fair amount of influence. He has a great relationship with the board. He has been and continues to be heavily involved in who is selected to be on the board. Although none of the board members are "yes-men", they get along very well and have relatively no conflict. They have been all on the same page, so to speak, in seeking God's will. The board allows the Senior Pastor to lead and offers a good balance to his frequently wild and crazy ideas. He willingly submits issues to them because he desires their accountability. He has never felt stifled or cramped by the board. While the board maintains the final veto power, the board grants the Senior Pastor freedom for most day-to-day decisions and he has never had a strong conviction squashed. The most the board has done in such cases is urge caution or adjustment, which has always been good input.

Riverside has a number of additional staff personnel. The Assistant Pastor, Paul, handles assimilation issues. This includes visitor follow-up, running the ALPHA program, and working with the Senior pastor on the Growth Group ministry. He is a vintage team player and has worked well with the Senior Pastor from day one without any incidents. He is a learner, a servant, and someone who wants all that God wants. The Church Administrator, Andy, primarily handles office details, but also provides additional administrative oversight to the building and the worship.

Present Challenges

While average attendance from 1995 (the year the church was planted by the Senior Pastor) through 1998 grew from 87 to 205, attendance since 1998 has either plateaued or slightly declined. The current year (2002) has seen a drop in average attendance to 191. While 2002 year giving fell slightly below budget, it should be noted that per capita general fund giving has risen from $14.36 to $19.24, the highest in the church's history, and general fund giving has risen from $1,255.00 to $3,679.00, the second highest giving in the church's history.

The board and staff perceive a definite leadership shortage within the church that needs to be addressed. Also, they are extremely dissatisfied with the lack of new converts, especially in light of their outreach programs, ALPHA, ESL, Overcomers Outreach, Artists Group and Growth Groups.

The church recently (May 2003) completed the NCD Survey. Note the following profile for RCC and especially their Minimum and Maximum factors.

Empowering Leadership:	72	MAX
Gift-Oriented Ministry:	55	MIN
Passionate Spirituality:	58	
Functional Structures:	60	
Inspiring Worship Services:	56	
Holistic Small Groups:	61	
Need-oriented Evangelism:	60	
Loving Relationships:	55	MIN

The church has formed an implementation team to begin working on their minimum factor. Although Holistic Small Groups rank high as a strength, the leadership team still sees a need to transition to a cell church paradigm. Is this wise? Should the church attempt simultaneously to engage in the NCD process and transition to a cell church paradigm? This can be accomplished with positive results if the transition decision making process employs the same biotic procedures as are employed in the decisions made relative to raising their minimum factor. Why would RCC desire to transition their small group system when it is as positive a force as it appears to be?

The reasons behind the desire to transition a strong holistic small group system becomes clearer if we recall a few basic facts Joel Barker stresses regarding paradigm shifts (Future Edge, 51). Recall for a moment his paradigm curve, drawn below.

The Paradigm Curve

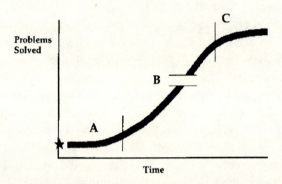

As RCC has perfected their current Growth Group system over the last few years, they have progressed up the paradigm curve in terms of problems solved. In particular, the level of edification their people experience is significantly higher than in the past. However, RCC is presently at a place on the paradigm curve (near the top) where their present small group paradigm can no longer efficiently solve the greatest problems they face, i.e. lack of new converts and raising up of new leaders. The cell church paradigm will be better able than their current small group paradigm to provide alternative solutions for those two problems, since cell groups by definition are evangelistically oriented and possess multiplicative DNA that mandates leadership development and empowerment.

Possible Solution Scenario

The transition to a more deliberate focused cell group ministry will begin with a four phase thrust. What will the four phases look like?

Phase 1 - Boot Camp I

Boot Camp is a process to help current church members possessing varying degrees of understanding about the cell church make the transition into cell life. Boot Camp provides an overview of the cell which is very practical and not merely theoretical. It serves as a bridge, helping many cross over from their current understanding of what the church is to what and how a cell church should function. While not attempting to duplicate what they will in the future experience once in a cell, Boot Camp will prepare them for entrance into that cell lifestyle. The average church member's traditional thinking acts as a filter, coloring everything they see and experience. There is thus a need to "re-program" their old thinking to a more Biblical understanding of the Body of Christ, in order to allow them to function properly in a cell group. Apart from the Boot Camp process, many who want to be in a cell would otherwise simply still not know how to participate in a healthy way. They would possess neither the understanding nor value base from which to move into the new cell lifestyle! The assumption of Boot Camp is that by combining teaching with experience and providing a safe environment in which people were encouraged and allowed to unpack their "baggage", the process of preparing members for healthy cell living will be hastened.

Having examined the Boot Camp process and material, RCC made the decision that no current members would be allowed to come into a cell without first processing through Boot Camp, much like the decision of the U.S. military toward raw recruits. On the other hand, new converts would would come into cells immediately, having been born into a new family. That which they lacked cognitively would be given to them at a later date as part of their on-going discipleship process.

In casting vision for the new cell ministry, Boot Camp would become an instrument for both addressing shortcomings and unattained goals in the present Growth Groups, and calling the church to a clearer standard of small group involvement and lifestyle. Those leading Growth Groups in the past have been unsure of their purpose and therefore how to reach it. Additionally, Growth Group attendance was sporadic, being considered optional by the members. Evangelistic outreach was minimal, and discipleship was occurring on a very limited basis, if at all. Boot Camp will help to recast and clarify the vision regarding basic cell ministry.

Chapter 5 ☞ *Learning to Think and Plan Biotically*

For additional information regarding Boot Camp, I suggest the reader contact Strategic Cell Ministries International (http://www.us.net/scmi). For an evaluation of Boot Camp, the reader is free to contact the Senior Pastor and/or staff at Riverside Community Church in Nutley, New Jersey.

The kickoff session for the first Boot Camp began February 5, 2003. Boot Camp I ran for twelve weeks through April 23rd. Those wishing to be future cell leaders and apprentices were invited to attend this initial Boot Camp. Some of those who participated were currently involved in leadership of one of the Growth Groups, others were not. Additional members who had no desire to actually lead a cell in the future but desired to become part of a future cell were also free to attend Boot Camp I. During this time the Groups were allowed to continue to meet on a weekly basis as they had in the past. However, some of the Growth Groups faced a leadership crisis and therefore were unable to continue. What caused such a crisis? The Growth Group's leader or leaders were not be able to manage both attending Boot Camp and continuing to lead their Growth Group. Such being the case, the Growth Groups found their leader(s) needing to give up leadership of the group in order to attend Boot Camp and the Growth Group therefore dissolved. Consequently, some Growth Group members opted to join Boot Camp I.

Phase 2 - Initial Prototype Cells

The Plan

Initial Prototype Cells were scheduled to begin to meet May 7th. How many initial Prototype Cells would begin would be based upon the number of Boot Camp graduates who had demonstrated they were ready to move into cell leadership and become the first fruit of cell leaders in the new cell structure. The Prototype Cell(s) would continue through the end of August. During their time in a Prototype Cell, those who would initially become leaders, as opposed to first generation interns, would also work through resource based training, receiving their cognitive cell leader instruction over an eight week period via training tapes and personalized follow-up. In essence, those who would become the pool for the first crop of leaders and apprentices in the new cell group structure would be on one track, and those who would initially be members of the cell groups would run on another track.

Real Life

Two initial prototype cells began to meet the week of May 11, 2003. The Head Coach led the Tuesday prototype. The Senior Pastor led the Wednesday prototype, which the Head Coach also attended. It should be noted here that without a Senior Pastor and Head Coach with previous cell church experience, two prototype cells would not have been attempted.

The Tuesday prototype began with nine members in addition to the Head Coach and spouse–three couples, one man, one woman, and one youth. A month into the prototype one of the key couples moved out of state due to an unforeseen change of jobs by the husband. The Wednesday prototype began with six members in addition to the Senior Pastor and Head Coach–three men and three women. Leadership training for those slated to become the 1st generation cell leaders was begun the week of July 14th. Training continued for eight weeks. The prototype launched four new cells the week of September 15th.

Phase 3 - Boot Camp II

The Plan

Boot Camp II was scheduled to commence on June 1st. Like the first Boot Camp, Boot Camp II would also go for 12 weeks and run through August 17. This Boot Camp would be open for all those desiring to be in a future cell. This second Boot Camp would cover essentially the same material as the first one. Boot Camp II would commence after the first Boot Camp was completed and would meet on a different night, in this case Sunday. It would be for all those who wished to be part of a Cell Group. Those who initially would be leading future cells would have already been through Boot Camp I and at this time would be receiving additional preparation in the Prototype Cell. This second Boot Camp would also allow those who missed any sessions from Boot Camp I to attend make-ups.

It was hoped that many, if not all, of those who had been attending Growth Groups would at this time switch over to Boot Camp. The

Growth Groups could continue to meet, if they chose to, or they could permanently disband if they preferred. Either way, all future training, equipping and coaching of leaders by the pastoral staff would come through the new cell structure. The cell groups would now become the primary place of pastoral care, equipping and discipling for all those who considered RCC to be their home church.

Growth Group leaders could continue to lead Growth Groups after the new cell structure was in place. However, those who continued to lead existing Growth Groups would also need to be in a cell group, Boot Camp being prerequisite. Also, as RCC transitions toward becoming a cell church, all those with corporate ministry would in time need to be members of the church.

Real Life

All of the Growth Groups but two disbanded and their members opted to become involved in Boot Camp II. Of the two Growth Groups that continued to meet, most of their members also attended Boot Camp II.

Phase 4 - Birthing the New Cells

The Plan

In September the new cells were slated to launch, along with an equipping track and coaching support system. The 1st generation cell leaders would be chosen from among those who had completed all of the training {Boot Camp I, Prototype Cell, and the cell leader intern training} and had demonstrated both a readiness to lead in this new paradigm and a personal lifestyle to support this new paradigm. The new cell groups would be working toward evangelizing the lost and seeking to multiply their group within a pre-designated time period. Each member of the cell, having already completed Boot Camp, would be expected to be actively participating not only in outreach to others, but also in personal equipping through the cell group.

RCC recognized that some may not choose to make the transition to cells at this time. No one would be forced to make the transition. There would still be many ways to be involved at RCC until the multiplication of the first cells. Opportunities for involvement would include ESL, Alpha, any remaining Growth Groups, Sunday School, Children's Ministry, Overcomers Outreach, Artists Group, etc.

Real Life

Four cells were born out of the two initial prototypes the second week of September. The original intent was to birth two mixed adult cells along with a men's cell and women's cell. In actual fact, two mixed adult cells, a men's cell and a women's cell were actually born.

Two Growth Groups have been allowed to continue. The Worship Team Growth Group will be disbanded by May of 2004 and the members filtered into then existing cells. The other Growth Group will be allowed to continue as is. In both cases, in order to not maintain parallel conflicting systems, the Growth Groups will receive no oversight, support, or recognition by RCC, and the level of pastoral care the members currently receive will not be increased.

Chapter 5 ☛ *Learning to Think and Plan Biotically*

PROCESSING A POSSIBLE SOLUTION - LEARNING TO THINK BIOTICALLY

The goal of RCC's cell transition is to glorify God, to see leaders empowered, to equip the saints for the work of service, to evangelize the lost and to participate fully in the Great Commission that had been entrusted to the church as God's people.

We have looked at the scenario RCC utilized to initially transition from Growth Groups to cell groups. From a cell standpoint, the decisions arrived at made good cell sense. Most cell churches would have stopped here. However, were the conclusions arrived at and the decisions made also biotic? Would they lead to "all by itself growth"? Could employing the principles of NCD add anything significantly to the decision making process and ultimate transition of RCC to a cell church? Could applying the biotic principles reveal potential problems now, so RCC would not have to face them later? Because RCC was also engaging in a process of implementing NCD, the leadership team was also challenged to run their cell decisions through an NCD biotic filter before they were implemented. What follows is a brief description of the thinking process RCC went through before actually implementing the above scenario.

As we attempt to apply the biotic principles to RCC's proposed course of beginning transition, we will employ a number of "guide questions" to stimulate our thinking. These guide guide questions are generic enough that they may be employed whenever a church has a specific decision it wants to make from a biotic perspective. The guide questions which follow have all been developed by Direction Ministry Resources, The Salvation Army (Australia Eastern Territory) and The Institute for Natural Church Development International for their PowerPoint presentation entitled *Biotic Principles*, and are included as part of the Biotic Principles Powerpoint Presentation Notes v1.0.

Biotic Principle #1: Interdependence

When seeking to apply the biotic principle of **Interdependence**, we are seeking to understand the answer to the question, "Are the long term effects that this step has on other areas of the church organism beneficial for the development of the church or not? (Implementation, 126)"

> **GUIDE QUESTION: INTERDEPENDENCE**
>
> **ARE THE INEVITABLE LONG TERM EFFECTS OF THIS DECISION TO CREATE BOOT CAMP BENEFICIAL FOR ALL THE AREAS OF THE CHURCH ORGANISM IMPACTED BY IT? (BIOTIC, 41)**

Because the church is an organism, RCC's leadership must consider how the church body will react as an organic whole. Allow me to borrow an illustration from medicine. When doctors prescribe medication, they must take into consideration side effects on the rest of the body. Steroids have been found in the short term to be highly beneficial to fight certain inflammations in the body. However, the impact on the thinking processes in some people, severe steroid psychosis– a chemically induced mental psychosis, must be considered before the medication is prescribed.

If RCC launches an initial twelve week cycle of Boot Camp, followed by a second Boot Camp cycle running simultaneously with a Prototype Cell, **what impact** will such action have on other ministries in the church? A follow-up to that question is to determine whether or not those impacts will be **good impacts long-term** for every ministry impacted. As good as Boot Camp and a Prototype Cell may appear to be, their impact on the overall church must be evaluated.

If these questions are not answered, then the Leadership team may well find themselves devoting remedial time and energy to such things as resolving internal conflicts, replacing Growth Group leaders burned out as they attempted to maintain an increased time schedule, or dealing with members who are leaving due to too much change too fast.

What ministries will be impacted by Boot Camp? What might be the short term & long term effects?

There are at least five ministries that will be impacted by the creation of the Boot Camp.

The first ministry to be effected will be ESL. In the short term, because of the limited facility space, childcare will pose an immediate conflict. The ESL will be meeting downstairs where the children would normally be provided for during Boot Camp. The issue of childcare for Boot Camp must be addressed. Boot Camp will also have a long term effect on ESL. As a result of the cells becoming functional throughout the body and the plan for each cell member to be released into body ministry based on their spiritual gifts discovered in and through the cell, the teacher pool available to teach the ESL classes will ultimately increase. However, in the interim period, there is an overlap between those who have taught and/or are teaching ESL and those who will be tapped as cell leaders. ESL will in the short term experience a decline in available teachers and might even have to be placed on hiatus for a period of time. Short term the effect of Boot Camp and the transition may be negative, although the longer term impact will be quite positive.

The second ministry to be impacted will be ALPHA. Boot Camp will run on Wednesday evening. ALPHA is run on Thursday evening. Unlike ESL, there should not be a conflict in facility scheduling between Boot Camp and ALPHA. However, the same situation does arise regarding the ALPHA leadership pool and cell leader pool as with the ESL teacher pool. In addition, the associate pastor and one board member both are involved leading ALPHA and will be involved leading cells. Their non-participation in ALPHA as a result of their involvement in cells could be crippling to the ALPHA ministry. On the other hand, should they continue serving with ALPHA while moving into cells, the additional time spent with ALPHA will impact significantly their time availability for relationship building during the twelve weeks of Boot Camp.

This leads to the impact on ministry number three, the adult Sunday School. Both men mentioned above also rotate teaching in the adult Sunday School. Additionally, a second Board member who also presently serves as a Growth Group leader and is being asked to join the Boot Camp also rotates as an adult Sunday School teacher. Thus, three out of four adult Sunday School teachers are being asked to initially become cell leaders, with the desire that they will also eventually move into positions as cell coaches. Can the adult Sunday School survive both in the short and long term?

Growth groups will endure the greatest impact. In the short term many of the present growth groups will cease to exist. Their leader will be asked to participate in the first Boot Camp cycle in preparation for becoming part of the prototype cell. If the growth group members become part of the first or second Boot Camp cycles, they will be ready to join the newly launched cells in September. Short term the edification they receive weekly through their group will cease. The slack can be picked by through Boot Camp relationships to some degree. In the long term, those who join a cell in September will receive greater care and discipleship, as well as having opportunity for greater service in the larger body of RCC.

What of those Growth Groups that choose to continue to meet during the summer? In the short term they will continue to receive and give as they have in the past. Pastoral care will not be lessened, but neither will it be increased. The long term effect, however, could be very negative. The groups will continue along a paradigm the church is choosing to reject, and, if they do not participate in Boot Camp, reject a paradigm shift the church is choosing to embrace. This sets up a possible adversarial position and the creation of great negative energy toward the transition process. It must be made crystal clear that all present Growth Groups will cease functioning upon the launch of the new cells in September.

The Youth Ministry will also be effected by Boot Camp. Both current Youth Growth Groups are led by adults. Optimally the four leaders will participate in Boot Camp and lead their youth to do the same. They may also continue to meet for the summer, lessening the effect of the changes taking place. The church has chosen the path of youth led cell groups. In the long term, this will radically effect the nature of the youth growth groups. The youth must step up to the plate and be trained as leaders. The current leaders must relinquish control and empower the youth. Short term this may eventuate in conflict of vision. If the new vision can be embraced, the long term result will be radically new youth cells. If the vision is resisted, because of the influence of the youth leaders, they could conceivably take the youth out of the mainstream vision of the church and kill a viable youth cell ministry at this point.

Finally, there will be a general fallout on all the ministries of the church. As a result of a time issue, some adults may be less involved on

Chapter 5 ☞ *Learning to Think and Plan Biotically*

Sunday due to their increased involvement in Boot Camp. This could have a negative short term impact on Children's Sunday School and Children's Church. Long term effect could be the same as that with ESL and ALPHA as regards teacher pool. The same possible benefits also accrue.

What ministries will be impacted by the Prototype Cell(s)? What might be the short term & long term effects?

Will moving the leaders out of Boot Camp and into prototype leadership cells create any additional impacts besides those already noted?

Those leaders who are wearing multiple ministry hats will have to begin to lighten their ministry plates. As lifestyle changes are made to allow for weekly relationship building among cell members and outreach to lost friends, they will feel a major time crunch. This will result in having to pare back other ministry involvement.

As three of the four current Adult Sunday School teachers begin to move into cell evangelism and cell leader training, they may well voice the need to end their teaching role in Sunday School. If they do so, in the short term the adult Sunday School may cease to function. Another prototype cell member is also a Children's Sunday School teacher. Her new duties as a cell intern may also impact her ability to continue teaching on Sunday mornings.

Summary Thoughts

It should be obvious by this exercise that although the decision to move the church toward Boot Camp and the leaders into a prototype cell this summer is a good decision regarding the cell transition, it is fraught with impact on the rest of the church, impact that must be considered and weighed before a final decision to proceed is reached.

Is the church willing to release current leaders from their commitments to ALPHA, ESL, and Sunday School so as to avoid leader burnout, even at the risk of impacting those ministries to the point of closure? Will the church opt to close all Growth Groups or allow them to function for an additional specified period as a parallel system? Understanding the long term impact, will RCC move the youth leaders and youth into Boot Camp this summer or allow them to resist the cell paradigm and continue with relatively independent sovereignty until a later date?

How will other biotic principles they impact RCC's decision toward implementing Boot Camp and a Prototype Cell?

Biotic Principle #2: Multiplication

When seeking to apply the biotic principle of **Multiplication**, we are seeking to understand the answer to the question, "Does this step contain multiplication dynamics or does it merely contribute to addition? (Implementation, 136)"

> **GUIDE QUESTION: MULTIPLICATION**
>
> HOW WILL THE CREATION OF BOOT CAMP ACTIVELY CONTRIBUTE TO THE MULTIPLICATION OF THE DISCIPLES, MINISTRIES, PROGRAMS AND GROUPS AFFECTED BY IT (BIOTIC, 43)

> **GUIDE QUESTION: MULTIPLICATION**
>
> HOW WILL WE UTILIZE OUR RESOURCES MORE EFFECTIVELY SO THAT THE DECISION TO CREATE BOOT CAMP WILL PRODUCE RESULTS WHICH MULTIPLY INDEFINITELY? (BIOTIC, 43)

Will Boot Camp be reproducible? If multiplication dynamics are not part and parcel of their proposal, asking this type of a question up front will cause the leadership of RCC to build multiplication dynamics into the DNA of Boot Camp before it is launched.

The initial cycle of Boot Camp will be taught and administered by the Senior Pastor. What plans will be put into place so that Boot Camp will raise up new leadership capable of facilitating and teaching future Boot Camp cycles, relieving the Senior Pastor of that responsibility and empowering additional leadership? Does the Senior Pastor understand that a major part of his role is to replicate himself in others so that Boot Camp will be able to expand? Does RCC's leadership understand that the purpose of Boot Camp is not simply to prepare present members for their transition into cells, but to prepare them in such a way that they bring into future Boot Camps friends who presently are choosing to opt out of the two Boot Camps being offered?

The same type of questions need to be raised regarding the prototype cell, although the answers are far more obvious, simply because of the pre-defined nature of the prototype cell. However, as an example of its importance, let's apply this multiplication dynamic to the training of those who will be part of the prototype cell(s).

Growth group leaders in the past have been trained and equipped to provide good pastoral care. However, they have, for the most part, neither reproduced themselves as leaders, nor have they multiplied their cells through any kind of evangelism. Without considering the multiplication dynamic at this point, present training would simply imitate the past. If multiplication dynamics are now built into the new prototype cell(s), then cell leader training and equipping will include practical instruction and skill sets to demonstrate how cell leaders may empower future cell members to ensure that new leadership will be constantly emerging. In addition, time and resources will be invested now in involving prototype cell members in active evangelism. Cell leaders will additionally be led to understand from the beginning that they will demonstrate their success as cell leaders primarily by raising up new leaders and multiplying their groups through evangelism.

Are multiplication dynamics built into Boot Camp?

Paul Kadlub presently serves as the Associate Pastor at RCC. Prior to bringing Twyla on staff to oversee the cell development, the goal was to ultimately train and release Paul as a staff cell pastor. Paul participated in the first Boot Camp, the plan being that he would begin to be trained to be able to lead a Boot Camp sometime in the future. There is in place a reproducible plan to train Paul, the long range effect being the creation of a reproducible plan to train future Boot Camp trainers as needed, all the while keeping in mind that Boot Camp facilitators/trainers need to be staff level with proven cell experience.

Paul is being utilized to help with logistics, to distribute electronic homework, and oversee the administrative details of Boot Camp I. He is being scheduled for two teaching times and accompanying evaluation during Boot Camp II. This was not done during Boot Camp I in order that Paul could experience one cycle as a full participant in every session of Boot Camp. The week following his teaching assignment he will handle the large group question and answer session dealing with the previous week's teaching and homework.To ensure his understanding is up to par, he will listen to the audio tapes from Boot Camp I for the sessions he is teaching and then be evaluated regarding his comprehension of their content. This cycle of hands-on training and evaluation will be continued until such time as Paul has the experience and expertise to totally lead a Boot Camp.

Are multiplication dynamics built into Prototype Cell(s)?

RCC has built multiplication dynamics into the prototype cell. The goal of the prototype is to multiply into four or five cells, each cell possessing a leader and at least one apprentice. This will be accomplished as leaders are developed through modeling, formal instruction, and informal instruction.

What is to be modeled will be defined both in qualitative and quantitative terms. These will include skills, understanding, and character qualities. Prototype cell members will experience cell life in all its dynamics during the initial phase of the prototype cell. They will be evaluated as to their cell participation, how they function in accountability relationships, how well they progress through their equipping track, their networking in the lives of their oikos members' lost friends, and how rapidly they are able to adapt life style changes. Those best demonstrating proven ministry will be asked to become the first generation cell leaders. The remainder will serve as apprentices during the first cell cycle. The last eight weeks of the prototype cell cycle, those selected as cell leaders will begin their formal equipping.

The formal equipping will be resource based rather than classroom based. The equipping process will include eight weeks of cell apprentice training tapes and accompanying assignments designed to tap into all three areas of learning, i.e. cognitive, affective, and psychomotor. A tape listening guide will accompany the training tapes containing a teaching outline, learning objectives, and discussion questions. The discussion questions will serve as the springboard for the future cell leader's one-on-one weekly time with their coach. As additional informal times are shared each week, it is hoped that learning will also happen in the midst of life's situations. The cell leaders in training will also begin to participate in leading the cell and in the formal debriefing times following cell meeting, during which times cell evaluations will be done.

Biotic Principle #3: Energy Transformation

When seeking to apply the biotic principle of **Energy Transformation**, we are seeking to understand the answer to the question, "Is this measure utilizing the energy relationships of the environment, or trying to fight them? (Implementation, 147)"

GUIDE QUESTION: ENERGY TRANSFORMATION

DOES THIS DECISION CONSIDER HOW ALL AVAILABLE ENERGY [POSITIVE AND NEGATIVE] WILL BE DIRECTED FOR STIMULATING GROWTH? (BIOTIC, 45)

GUIDE QUESTION: ENERGY TRANSFORMATION

HOW WILL WE FOCUS THE UNHARNESSED RESOURCES TOWARD ACHIEVING THE DESIRED OUTCOME? (BIOTIC, 45)

The changes being instituted by RCC are significant in the life of the church. People will not feel ambivalent toward them. They will have strong feelings one way or the other. When RCC announces these changes, all sorts of reactions will be encountered.

Does the leadership team understand what energy (positive and negative) will be generated by the mandatory nature of Boot Camp, the ultimate death of the Growth Group ministry, and the demands upon those asked to participate in the prototype cell(s)? Does the leadership team have a plan to

Natural Church Development and Cell Church - Friends or Foes?

build upon positive energies created by the proposed transition? Does the leadership team have a plan to turn around negative reactions so that instead of being destructive to the forward movement and growth of the church, they become positive healthy forces? Is RCC's leadership aware of unused positive resources within their midst?

Positive energies needing to be channeled?

The majority of individuals coming out of Boot Camp I had high, very positive energy levels regarding what they experienced. One way of channeling that energy could be to give them time each Sunday morning to share with the congregation their testimony regarding what they experienced and how they had benefited from Boot Camp. Their energy could then be utilized to fire up others to sign up for Boot Camp II. It was decided not to utilize their testimonies in this way because the sign up for Boot Camp II was already at the maximum level. Their testimonies would then over promote what we could not deliver.

Two men in particular who had recently been part of ALPHA had experienced increased excitement as a result of their ALPHA involvement. Previously, RCC has experienced little success at conserving the fruit coming out of ALPHA. The next logical step for these men following ALPHA is involvement in cell life. The excitement of these two men now has been channeled into Boot Camp and into their new cells.

Negative energy needing redirection, not combat?

An example at this point would be in order to help illustrate how negative energy can be identified and redirected. The youth ministry at RCC provides such an example.

It was the desire of the leadership at RCC to transition the youth, like their parents, into cell life. The youth ministry had for a long time been given a fair amount of autonomy. There was no youth pastor on staff. When it was learned that the leadership team desired to transition both adults and youth to cells via Boot Camp, resistance arose on the part of the lay youth leadership. A meeting was held between the Senior Pastor, cell consultant/NCD coach, Head Coach, and the youth leaders to help dissipate the negative energies and steer the youth leadership (and thus the youth) toward Boot Camp. The meeting, while positive and alleviating some fears, still did not "convince" the youth leadership that either Boot Camp or cell life would be a more positive experience than what they were already experiencing. At this point many cell churches would have simply forced the issue. After all, the church was moving toward cells and the youth leadership should not be allowed to "do its own thing" and not embrace the new move of God, especially since it was lay led.

RCC's Senior leadership decided against assuming a combative stance and directly fighting the intransigence. Employing the biotic principle of energy transformation, a way was sought to redirect the negative energy. The primary youth leader was asked to become not only a part of the first Boot Camp, but also a part of the initial prototype cell. A second youth leader was asked to become part of the second Boot Camp. Their negative energies were redirected into the Boot Camp process. During the twelve weeks of Boot Camp, fears and apprehensions could begin to be answered. The prototype cell would demonstrate the reality of what otherwise was only considered to be theoretical. In the interim, no changes were to be made to the youth ministry.

What has been the result? Both youth leaders have now been assimilated into the first generation cells. The second leader noted above is presently being trained as an intern in the men's cell. Both are sold on cell life. They have recently come back to RCC's leadership and are requesting a youth Boot Camp to prepare the youth for release into cell life. The negative energies, rather than being combated, were redirected and transformed into positive energies that now are propelling the youth ministry and church forward in its transition to cells.

Sources of untapped positive energy in need of harnessing?

There is an implicit assumption in the proposal that the new cell leaders will arise from the current crop of Growth Group leaders. Could there be other members of RCC who have not been Growth Group leaders in the past, but who have a strong desire to be a cell leader under the new paradigm? The energy contained within such members will remain untapped and possibly go to waste if there is no way to enlist them as part of the prototype cell(s). They are an untapped source of energy within the church that could propel the church forward.

Natural Church Development and Cell Church - Friends or Foes?

Upon reflection, the leadership at RCC identified two couples that were not presently Growth Group leaders but had significant potential as cell leaders. Both couples were excited about the transition. One of the couples had continued attending the church primarily due to the change of direction announced months earlier as the Senior Pastor began to prepare the church for transition. Both couples were new to the church and area. They possessed energies that were hitherto simply untapped. A decision was made to invite these individuals into the prototype cells. One of the couples is now together leading an adult cell. The husband of the other couple is an apprentice for the men's cell. Both are fully committed to cell life.

Biotic Principle #4: Multi-Usage

When seeking to apply the biotic principle of **Multi-usage**, we are seeking to understand the answer to the question, "Do the results of this measure further sustain this ministry, or do we have here only a one-way street? (Implementation, 156)"

> **GUIDE QUESTION: MULTI-USAGE**
>
> HOW WILL THE OUTCOMES OF THIS DECISION LEAD THIS MINISTRY, PROGRAM OR ACTIVITY TO BECOME INCREASINGLY SELF-SUSTAINING? (BIOTIC, 47)

> **GUIDE QUESTION: MULTI-USAGE**
>
> WHAT RESOURCES WILL THIS MINISTRY, PROGRAM OR ACTIVITY DEVELOP FOR ITS ONGOING GROWTH? (BIOTIC, 47)

Certain resources must be allocated for the initial startup of both Boot Camp and the prototype cell(s). Are there additional situations that these resources may be applied to? How can Boot Camp and the prototype cell(s) develop to the point that they no longer require outside resourcing? In what ways can they eventually generate their own resources?

Boot Camp Resources - Personnel

There are a number of ways that personnel can be used to help Boot Camp become self-sustaining. Graduates from Boot Camp can participate and become a small group facilitator in future Boot Camp cycles. They also can be given opportunity to give public testimony regarding the benefits of their equipping and accountability experiences. Graduates might also participate in future Boot Camp cycles in order to build relationships with those going through Boot Camp with a view to assimilating these new people into their group. Cell leaders can return to Boot Camp to give testimony regarding how Boot Camp led to their leading of cells.

Boot Camp Resources - Material

The course curriculum for Boot Camp has been set. As a result, the PowerPoint presentations are utilized from Boot Camp to Boot Camp. The presentations can also be utilized in presenting Boot Camp to others, explaining various aspects of Boot Camp, reinforcing to cell members later what may have slipped in practice as well as made available for make-up sessions. The homework assignments provide excellent teaching and preaching material on such subjects as community, the cross, the church as the family of God, evangelism, and edification.

Boot Camp Resources - Time

The time spent in building relationships in Boot Camp can be turned around and built upon as the members move together into cell life. The accountability patterns can be carried over into the new cells. The habit patterns established and the consistency with equipping will be the basis for future equipping as the members are released and moved into corporate ministry with its own attendant equipping track. The change in values relating to time, ministry and the lost will effect the Boot Camp graduates in all the areas in which they find themselves ministering in the future.

Prototype Cell Resources - Personnel

Prototype cell members will become apprentices and eventually become leaders in the future cells. Some will undoubtedly also go on to become coaches. The skills they acquire in small group dynamics through the training in the prototype can be utilized in any of the meeting settings they may find themselves in as future leaders in the church. The values change they undergo in the prototype as their lifestyles are stretched and transformed will also carry over into every aspect of ministry. Future evangelism will be affected as a result of their new awareness and understanding/adopting of oikos network principles.

Prototype Cell Resources - Material

Many of the forms they are trained to use in the prototype they will use later in their cells and be able to pass on their usage to their apprentices. Thus the Training Tracker that tracks accountability and equipping consistency and faithfulness as well as the Hosting lists can be used in future cells. The equipping books through which they have been mentored now become a record of their personal journey and history that can be shared with future disciples. The cell guides and prototype templates provide the pattern for future cells without the need to redesign the wheel each cell cycle. The song pool selected by those leading worship can be carried over to other cells. In addition, because the cell song pool is a subset of the church's larger song pool, familiarity of the songs will be increased, resulting in a more worshipful environment being created on Sunday as people are freed from the struggle of worshipping with songs they do not know or with which they are unfamiliar.

Chapter 5 ☞ *Learning to Think and Plan Biotically*

Biotic Principle #5: Symbiosis

When seeking to apply the biotic principle of **Symbiosis**, we are seeking to understand the answer to the question, "Does this step contribute to fruitful cooperation of different forms of ministry, or does it promote ecclesiastical monoculture? (Implementation, 167)"

> **GUIDE QUESTION: SYMBIOSIS**
>
> HOW DOES THIS DECISION ACTIVELY PROMOTE COOPERATION BETWEEN DIVERSE GROUPS AND INDIVIDUALS IN THE CHURCH TO ACHIEVE THEIR HEALTHY GROWTH? (BIOTIC, 49)

> **GUIDE QUESTION: SYMBIOSIS**
>
> WHAT DIVERSE RESOURCES WILL BE BROUGHT TOGETHER IN A MUTUALLY BENEFICIAL WAY? HOW WILL THAT BE DONE? (BIOTIC, 49)

Symbiosis celebrates the diversity within the body of Christ and encourages cooperative ministry between different parts of the body. Symbiosis also recognizes that there is a greater growth potential for RCC as the differing ministries are brought together than if they remained separate. Therefore, RCC must answer the question, "What other ministries would benefit from working alongside of Boot Camp?" Synergy is released as ministries cooperate and get together. What other ministries would Boot Camp benefit from working alongside of? So that Boot Camp will not be perceived as an isolated ministry, how will other areas of the church be encouraged to work with Boot Camp? In other words, what connections can be encouraged between Boot Camp and the rest of the church? In what ways can other ministries become involved with Boot Camp? Who needs to facilitate these connections?

What other ministries would benefit from working alongside of Boot Camp and the Prototype Cell(s)? What other ministries would Boot Camp and the Prototype Cell(s) benefit from working alongside of?

Boot Camp would benefit from working alongside of the Worship Ministry. The staff is wanting to have worship prior to the actual start of the Boot Camp each week. Boot Camp would benefit greatly if those who were attending Boot Camp and were also part of the Worship Ministry led worship during these times. If no worship personnel were part of Boot Camp, then there is the opportunity for those in the worship ministry to come and lead anyway as an expression of their support for Boot Camp as well as their ministry gifting.

Boot Camp, ALPHA and the prototype would all benefit from partnering together. Boot Camp would provide ALPHA with a way of enfolding new Christians immediately back into the church. ALPHA could provide those in the prototype an avenue for oikos evangelism. Boot Camp provides the door for entrance into the prototype and future cells.

In what ways can other ministries become involved with Boot Camp?

The Care Ministry can come alongside of Boot Camp. The Care Ministry teams are the first contacts visitors have with RCC. They greet them at the service and do the follow up the next week. Boot Camp provides an avenue for visitors to get involved with the ministry of RCC and learn what the church is about. Those in the Care Ministry can direct visitors to Boot Camp.

The Bagel Ministry could contribute the bagels left over from Sunday to the Boot Camp ministry for use during the fellowship time instead of throwing out the bagels after Sunday's services.

Chapter 5 ☛ *Learning to Think and Plan Biotically*

Biotic Principle #6: Functionality

When seeking to apply the biotic principle of **Functionality**, we are seeking to understand the answer to the question, "Is this measure producing fruit for the kingdom of God, or is it missing its purpose? (Implementation, 176)"

GUIDE QUESTION: FUNCTIONALITY

WHAT MEASURABLE STATEMENT OF PURPOSE - PROMOTING HEALTHY GROWTH - IS INCLUDED IN THIS DECISION? (BIOTIC, 51)

GUIDE QUESTION: FUNCTIONALITY

HOW WILL THE LEADERSHIP CONTINUE TO ENSURE THAT THE ALLOCATED RESOURCES ARE EFFECTIVELY CONTRIBUTING TO HEALTHY GROWTH? (BIOTIC, 51)

Obviously, Boot Camp and the Prototype Cell(s) are being initiated for a specific purpose. What are the measurable goals that the leadership team have agreed upon for Boot Camp? For the Prototype Cell(s)? Who is responsible for Boot Camp I achieving its goal? Boot Camp II? The Prototype Cell(s)? What accountabilities are being established prior to release of either ministries? The statements of purpose will become the yardsticks by which the effectiveness of both Boot Camp and the Prototype Cell(s) will be measured. Are the ministries resulting in healthy fruit? What dates have been set for review. While there should be a final review, there must also be ongoing reviews to ensure the ministries are functioning properly and progressing in a timely manner toward fulfillment of their goal(s).

Statement of Purpose - Boot Camp

The purpose of Boot Camp is to help church members who are interested in becoming functional members of cells transition into cell life. The goal is that 95% of those who complete the first three weeks also complete the entire Boot Camp and that 90% of those finishing become involved immediately in a cell.

Evaluation Dates - Boot Camp

Boot camp will be evaluated following the third week and following the final 12th week. The percent of those dropping out and those entering into cells will be calculated.

Statement of Purpose - Prototype Cell(s)

The purpose of the prototype cell is to communicate visually to the members at RCC a holistic small group that is fully functional in the areas of edification, equipping, evangelism, empowering leaders, and releasing every member into corporate ministry.

Evaluation Dates - Prototype Cell(s)

Edification is to be evaluated week to week after the cell meeting during the debriefing time with the prototype cell leadership.

Progress along the equipping track is to be evaluated monthly through the use of the Training Tracker form. Also, regularity in meeting with their equipping partner will be evaluated each week, also through the use of the Training Tracker form.

Evangelism will be evaluated as to whether or not the prototype cell stays on track with the weekly cell guides.

The last eight weeks of the prototype cell is given to empowering and releasing leaders. How well each week's lesson is learned will be judged as those tapped as 1st generation cell leaders practice leading the different parts of cell and work through their training material.

On the one hand, due to the shortened life cycle of the prototype, it will not be possible for the participants to work through the entire equipping track to the point where every member could be released into their gifted ministry. On the other hand, each of the members in the prototype is there because their corporate ministry is felt to be leading a cell.

Chapter 5 — Learning to Think and Plan Biotically

Conclusions

We have spent a great deal of time attempting to implement the biotic principles into the decision making process at RCC before launching Boot Camp and the Prototype Cell(s). What will be the end results of all of our efforts?

Interdependence: **Positively Impacting RCC's other ministries**

Multiplication: **Growing and reproducing**

Energy Transformation: **Energies focused toward growth**

Multi-usage: **Moving toward self-sufficiency**

Symbiosis: **Working together with other ministries**

Functionality: **Held accountable and fulfilling its purpose**

Why engage in this process? It might do well to restate our "bottom line" mentioned earlier. As we learn to make better and better decisions using the biotic principles, blockages to growth will be anticipated and removed, our resources will be more effectively allocated, and **we will be actively cooperating with God to maximize our church's potential for "all by itself" healthy growth.**

6

LEARNING TO EVALUATE BIOTICALLY

BUT EXAMINE EVERYTHING CAREFULLY; HOLD FAST TO THAT WHICH IS GOOD; 1 THESS. 5:21

OBSERVE HOW THE LILIES OF THE FIELD GROW... MATT. 6:28

BUT LET EACH ONE EXAMINE HIS OWN WORK... GAL 6:4

Chapter 6 ☞ *Learning to Evaluate Biotically*

THE CHALLENGE BEFORE US

I am attempting to accomplish with this chapter what I do not think has been attempted by others before me. I will be walking the reader through the actual process undertaken in the creation of two prototype cells, as well as their planned and actual multiplication.

In the following pages the reader will be introduced to the leadership of each prototype cell as well as to each of the prototype cell members. The reader will gain insight into the thinking of the Head Coach, who, in conjunction with the Senior Pastor, dreamed with Jesus of a better tomorrow and planned how to arrive there.

The events described below in *Life Happens* are actual events experienced by the members of the prototype cells. Cell life is biotic, not mechanical and artificial. As a result, life does happen. As life happens, it often redirects the best laid plans of mice and men. While unforeseen by us, the future is known by the Eternal One who holds our future in His hands. Knowing this, we are undeterred by that which befalls us in the execution of our plans. As Solomon once noted in Proverbs 16:33, "The lot is cast into the lap, but its every decision is from the Lord."

Having been privy to the original plans, the reader will find instructive the final outcome detailed in *And It Came to Pass*. The outcome is not always what we expect or plan for! If we were building a robot instead of growing a church, we could stick to the plans. However, growth demands adjustment and flexibility. As noted throughout this book, church growth is biotic, not mechanical. There are some things men can do, i.e. remove the blockages to growth, prepare the soil, plant the seed, and go to sleep. Growth comes from the Lord of the harvest. It cannot be manufactured by field workers.

An unknown author once said, "That which we expect we must inspect." In keeping with that wisdom, the conclusion of this chapter will be an inspection and evaluation of the prototype multiplication process from both a cell perspective and biotic NCD perspective. As a result of this rather lengthy process, it is my sincere desire that you, the reader, may benefit both by the successes gained and the lessons learned.

I am indebted to the staff of Riverside Community Church and to each of the members of the two prototype cells, all of whom have given me the release to freely describe the process and circumstances through which we together walked during the four month prototype cell life cycle.

In the Beginning...

Prototype Cell Leadership - Getting Acquainted

Don Flynn is the Senior Pastor of Riverside Community Church in Nutley, New Jersey. Riverside is part of the Christian & Missionary Alliance fellowship, having its beginning nearly ten years ago as a church restart in 1994. Don has been the Senior Pastor since that initial restart. For a number of years RCC had a small group ministry, Growth Groups, that unfortunately failed to raise up leaders and multiply. Having studied the cell paradigm thoroughly, Don is now committed both to moving the church into a cell paradigm and employing the principles of NCD to assist the church in healthy development. He functioned as the cell leader for the prototype cell which met on Wednesday evenings at 7:30.

Twyla Brickman came on staff with RCC in May of 2003. Twyla was on staff with Faith Community Church in Grand Forks, North Dakota as the church originally transitioned to cells from 1986-1994. Twyla served in the areas of worship, administration, and cell development. She served as part of TOUCH Outreach Ministries developing their conference department, administrating and teaching at *The Year of Transition*, and regularly teaching conferences. She was on staff with Hope Christian Church as a Trainer/Consultant/Pastor and oversaw the development of of the Women's zone at HCC. She has also participated in the training of hundreds of pastors and leaders in Russia, where she lived and worked with her husband in St. Petersburg, Russia. She co-pastored a cell plant in Overland Park, Kansas before coming to Riverside. Twyla is a graduate of Regent University, earning a Masters degree with an emphasis in Cell Church. Her mandate at Riverside is to assist the Senior Pastor in planning the transition of RCC, overseeing the day-to-day transition, and empowering and equipping cell leadership. Twyla served as the cell leader for the prototype cell which met on Tuesday evenings. She was also part of the Wednesday prototype cell, assisting Don and encouraging his development.

This author was a member of both prototype cells, serving behind the scenes in an advisory capacity to both Twyla and Don, while at the same time functioning up front as a regular cell member.

Chapter 6 ☛ *Learning to Evaluate Biotically*

Tuesday Prototype Cell Members - Getting Acquainted

Dave and Maki Evans

Dave and Maki Evans are former Growth Group leaders. Dave works in the medical field. Maki has her own business as a make-up artist. Maki came to this country from the Philippines to study. While in school she and Dave met and eventually married.

Roland and Naomi Urgino

At the time of their involvement in the prototype cell, Roland and Naomi Urgino were not yet members of RCC. They had visited the church at the end of 2002 and remained after learning that the pastor was moving the church toward a cell paradigm. Roland is a graduate of the International School of Theology in California and has been involved in church planting since 1995. Naomi has worked both secular employment and for Campus Crusade. Neither of them had been members of one of RCC's Growth Groups. Through the NCD process, Roland and his wife were identified as a source of untapped energy and therefore asked to become part of Boot Camp I with a view to having them in the prototype cell and eventually leading a cell. Roland and Naomi are from a Philippine background.

Ed and Debbie Woodward

Ed and Debbie Woodward have been members of Riverside ??? years. At the time he was asked to participate in the prototype, Ed was also serving on the Board at RCC, rotating teaching assignments with three other men for the adult Sunday school and together with his wife leading a Bible Study one night during the week. Ed and Debbie were also former Growth Group leaders. Ed and Debbie have three grown children who still live at home. Ed works for UPS while Debbie manages the home.

Paul Kadlub

Paul originally came to RCC as a student intern from Alliance Theological (ATS) seminary in Nyack, New York. Having completed his internship, he was asked to stay and come on board as Associate Pastor. Paul also heads up the Care Ministry and ALPHA program at RCC. His desire is to eventually be sent abroad with the C&MA Mission Board. In moving toward that goal, Paul's wife, Mary, is working currently toward the completion of her own degree at ATS. Due to her full time employment, Mary was unable to participate in Boot Camp I. She participated in Boot Camp II while Paul was in the prototype cell.

Nancy Stabinsky

Nancy Stabinsky has been a member of Riverside ??? years. Her husband, Mark, is not a member of RCC, regularly attending instead a local Catholic Church. Their youngest son, Adam is a member of the youth group. Their oldest son, Eric, is with the Nutley police. Nancy serves as the anchor for the Youth Group at RCC. Though not originally in favor of moving the youth as a group into Boot Camp and cells, Nancy has herself moved through Boot Camp and into the prototype cell.

Rebekah Giffone

Rebekah Giffone is fifteen years old. Rebekah is neither a member of the church nor presently a member of the youth group. She is being home schooled and is part of a completely different oikos network. She was very much interested in the cell concept and, what is notable, Rebekah voluntarily chose to attend Boot Camp I by herself, even though her parents, regular RCC attendees, were not in Boot Camp.

Wednesday Prototype Cell Members - Getting Acquainted

Mike Jetton

Mike Jetton has been a member of RCC from its inception in 1994. Mike, a former Growth Group leader, is also a Board member at Riverside. Mike lives and works in another community a good 30+ minutes driving time from the church. Mike has known the pastor since childhood and came to the Lord soon after Don did. Mike's wife is not involved at this time, caring for their two young children.

Ed Woodward III

Ed Woodward III is the son of Ed and Debbie Woodward and has led a Growth Group previously. When Boot Camp I began, Ed III joined Boot Camp while continuing to lead his Growth Group. Ed III, single and still liv-

Chapter 6 ☛ *Learning to Evaluate Biotically*

ing at home, is an artist, having a number of his pieces of artwork published in children's books.

Andy Jelliffe

Andy Jelliffe is on staff full time as the Administrator at Riverside. He and his wife, Kathy, have two young girls. Kathy is on Riverside's NCD Implementation Team and Missions Committee. In light of her other responsibilities and knowing her calling is not to lead a cell, she chose not to become part of the prototype cell along with her husband, but participated in Boot Camp II.

Amelia Whipple

Amelia Whipple has only been a Christian a few years. She is an early adopter, and as such was ready for the prototype. She and her husband, Bob, have one young grade school child whom she home schools. Bob is part of the national Overcomers Outreach Ministry and leads an Overcomers group at the church. Bob, a Viet Nam veteran, has experienced the severe and debilitating results of exposure to agent orange. As a result, he is unable to participate in as much as he might otherwise like. For a number of reasons, then, he was unable to participate in the prototype, but did attend Boot Camp.

Leigh Flynn

Leigh Flynn is the pastor's wife. Leigh and Don have three children, their youngest being under two. Leigh oversees the nursery at the church.

Connie Hayes

Connie Hayes is a strong Christian woman. She and her husband, David, have four children. Connie is another stay at home mom who also home schools her children. David works at the New York Rescue Mission. Due in part to his work hours and commute, David stayed with the children during Boot Camp I to allow his wife to attend. He is attending Boot Camp II while Connie is in the prototype.

Ellen DiStefano

Ellen DiStefano worked for years in New York City. She is now at home with their two children where she also runs a scrapbooking business.

Ellen attended Boot Camp I while her husband kept the children. Ellen and Joe were not members of Riverside at the point they were asked to become a part of the prototype. Once again, the NCD process led to the conclusion that here was untapped potential energy. Joe completed Boot Camp II.

Envisioning the Big Picture - Dreaming with Jesus

Established Relationships

What was the thinking behind the decisions that led to the formation of the two prototypes? Why break them into the two groups with the composition as noted above?

Don had begun teaching Boot Camp I prior to Twyla's and the author's arrival on staff at RCC. Since he was not sure who would become future leaders, a general invitation was offered with far more attending than would normally be suggested. Two prototypes were selected over the creation of a single prototype due to the number of potential leaders that sprang forth. Twenty people in a prototype cell would have been unrealistic. Small group dynamics required the creation of two small groups, not one large group. It was felt that Don and Twyla could handle two prototype cells. Normally one prototype is established, not two. For additional information on prototype development, see *Preparing the 21st Century Church*. When we examined how the division could be made, the leadership team looked at the relationships already naturally established and attempted to form the prototypes along those lines.

The Desire of the Heart

The desire of RCC's leadership team was to form cells employing a pure Jethro model. Don would function within that structure as the initial Captain of 100. Twyla would serve as a Captain of 50 over four, possibly five cells.

As originally envisioned, the desire was that the cell leadership would be distributed as follows. Ed and Debbie would lead a mixed adult cell with Dave and Maki as their apprentices. Roland and Naomi would lead a second mixed adult cell with Paul and Mary serving as their apprentices. Mike, Ed III and Andy would form a men's cell, Mike being the cell leader. Amelia would form a women's cell, her apprentices being Ellen, Leigh and Connie. There was also the anticipation that Nancy and Rebekah would form a prototype youth girl's cell. However, we have learned through experience that all cell plans must be firmly set in jello.

With the departure of the Evans, the vision needed to be refocused. Ed and Debbie Woodward would still possibly lead a mixed adult cell, but with Andy and if possible, Kathy Jelliffe as their apprentices. Roland and Naomi would now serve as cell leaders in a mixed adult cell, their apprentices becoming Joe and Ellen Distefano. It was hoped that Joe, although he was in Boot Camp II and not the prototype, would agree to serve alongside his wife as an apprentice. Paul and Mary Kadlub would lead the final mixed adult cell, David and Connie Hayes serving in the capacity of their apprentices. David, like Joe, was in Boot Camp II and not the prototype. Amelia would serve as a woman's cell leader with Leigh as her apprentice. Sonia, a graduate of Boot Camp II, would possibly be in the wings as another apprentice. Leigh's desire was to eventually lead a daytime women's cell for new mothers. Mike would still form a men's cell with Ed III as his apprentice. It was still anticipated that Nancy would lead a prototype youth cell for young girls, Rebekah being released as her apprentice and eventually becoming a youth cell leader.

Whether or not the cells to be launched in September would develop as hoped, would depend upon the proven ministry of those within the two prototype cells and those coming out of Boot Camp II. The mixture was still jello gelling. In the end, God would jiggle the jello again in a sovereign way.

Proactively Planning and Moving Toward Multiplication

It is a principle of life that all living things grow and multiply. To not grow and multiply is to be consigned to death. While growth and multiplication cannot be manufactured, there are things that we can do to create a healthy environment in which life can flourish. In this way we can proactively plan and move toward multiplication.

If we desire a prototype cell to be in actuality the first model of that which we desire to reproduce, we best help the model to be all that it should be. Toward that end Twyla proactively moved the cell forward in the areas of edification, equipping, evangelism, and empowering. I say proactively, because it was not left to haphazard chance, but systematically planned. Did the plan need adjustment? Certainly it did. We are working with living, breathing people, and people are not mechanical robots that operate on que. But this has never stopped God from planning.

Natural Church Development and Cell Church - Friends or Foes?

Many of the principles of healthy edification were taught in bite size pieces to the prototype cell members in the context of ministry. Sometimes they were formally explained, while at other times they modeled and then interpreted. Did the cells experience edification? You bet they did, week to week. The Wednesday prototype had real life opportunity when during the first week of its life the sibling of one of its members committed suicide. Later that same cell was to have additional opportunity as the spouse of one of its members underwent emergency brain surgery. The cell members needed to experience laying hands on one another, praying for one another, and allowing the Christ who dwelt within them to reach out and touch those around them, lost and saved alike.

Equipping was not left up to chance either. The leadership had carefully selected a basic equipping track all cell members would progress through. Their progress was tracked through the use of a *Training Tracker* form and a cell *Passport*.

How do you move people who have either never, or rarely evangelized, to the place of building relationships with lost people and developing those relationships on a weekly basis? Such movement does not happen in a vacuum. A comprehensive plan was put in place and implemented week by week until outreach to the unbelieving became part of a lifestyle. While we cannot make someone come to Christ, we can create a favorable environment in which God can touch people and birth them into His Kingdom. We can proactively help people to move along a change continuum in the area of evangelism.

The issue of future leadership is a problem for every cell church. The leadership pool usually appears small. However, people can be empowered and when trained, released into leadership. The Growth Group paradigm had changed. What had made many of these prototype cell members good leaders in the old paradigm would not necessarily make them good cell leaders in the new cell paradigm. In other words, everything went back to zero. These who would be the first of a long line of future leaders somehow must gain the knowledge, skills and heart for the work before them. As a consequence, they must be empowered and trained in way that would be reproducible in future cells. This mechanism was also proactively set into place. These cell apprentices were examined for development and proven ministry in the following areas.

Chapter 6 ☞ *Learning to Evaluate Biotically*

Proven Ministry Stage 1 - Accountability Partners

The prototype cell members had already experienced accountability relationships in Boot Camp. Their faithfulness in meeting had been tracked. When accountability relationships were set up in the prototype cell, the process attempted to take note of and honor the already existing relationships, rather than forcing new relationships. How faithful and consistent the cell members were was observed. Those faithful in little can be trusted with much. Those not faithful in little need additional opportunity for proven ministry.

Proven Ministry Stage 2 - Let the Cream Rise

Cream will always rise to the top. Those who were to serve as the first cell leaders it was believed would also rise to the top. A number of factors was scrutinized. As noted above, faithfulness in accountability relationships was one factor. How well each individual entered into community life through the week was also noted, as well as how they began to interact with those lost individuals for whom the cell was praying and reaching out. Community and outreach were gauges of an aspirational cell lifestyle becoming more integrated. Cell members' sensitivity during ministry both to the Spirit and toward those to whom they ministered, as well as their active participation during ministry opportunities were also taken into consideration.

Proven Ministry Stage 3 - Tag, You're It

There came the point when a decision had to be made regarding who would be asked to become initial cell leaders. These individuals and couples were then formally interviewed and asked to consider becoming the first generation cell leaders. Most answered in the affirmative and immediately began their formal cognitive and psycho-motor training.

Proven Ministry Stage 4 - Formal Instruction / Coaching

The leadership team decided not to have a formal apprentice training class. Rather than go the route of classroom instruction, RCC determined that a more reproducible and adaptable methodology would be to employ resource based training. Each cell leader's weekly training was provided with a cell leader training tape and corresponding listening guide (visit http://www.us.net/scmi). The listening guide provided the apprentice with a teaching outline to follow and to fill in where appropriate, a set of learning objectives for each teaching, as well as a set of discussion questions that would be covered one-on-one with their coach at some point during the week. This process allowed for greater freedom on the part of the apprentice. They were free to listen and takes notes at their leisure on their schedule. The one-on-one coaching facilitated deeper relationship building between apprentice and coach and allowed for more personal interaction and evaluation of their understanding. The attempt was made to integrate the meeting times into a normal apprentice lifestyle. Thus, meetings were done over coffee, over lunches, over dinners, or as part of recreational times together.

Proven Ministry Stage 5 - Hands-on Equipping

The hands-on equipping was done in the cell week to week. The apprentices were assigned various parts of the cell to lead, coordinated with their formal tape instruction. This was done under the watchful eye and care of the cell leader. This would also provide a model for the apprentice for future training of their own apprentices. Following each cell meeting, the cell leader and apprentices would meet 30-45 minutes for a time of debriefing. What and why the cell leader did what they did would be interpreted. A cell report form was used to evaluate each part of the cell meeting (welcome, worship, word, works). The apprentices were asked to rate on a scale of 1-5 the effectiveness of the part they led. They were then asked what they felt they could have done to have brought it to the next level. A cell apprentice is generally harder on themselves than would be the cell leader! Their self evaluation placed the cell leader in the position of being an encourager, rather than a corrector.

LIFE HAPPENS

The Curse of a Mobile Society - Career Moves

Soon after the prototype began, we were confronted with the possibility of losing a key couple, Dave and Maki Evans. Although Dave and Maki had lived in the area for a number of years, had put down roots and had strong friendships, Dave's employer was going through a major struggle within the industry and Dave could see the handwriting on the wall in regards to the company's future and his place in it. He had contacts with a company in Philadelphia. He brought to the cell the situation with which he was faced.

Chapter 6 ☛ Learning to Evaluate Biotically

We prayed with them as they put out feelers and sought the Lord's direction. In the end, they both felt that it was the Lord's will for them to move to Philadelphia. That was a significant blow to the prototype and its projected multiplication. Both Dave and Maki had potential not only as cell leaders, but as coaches. Back to the prayer room and drawing board!

A Thief in the Night - Brain Tumors

The time had arrived for the formal selection of those who would become the first cell leaders when the prototype multiplied. Connie had been in the prototype; David had not. However, David was completing Boot Camp II, and it was felt that together with his other experience and background, David and Connie made a strong team and could together do a great job of being apprentices in one of the new cells. Twyla visited with the couple on July 31, 2003. She left there about 10:00 p.m. that evening, asking the Hayes to pray over their decision. Within five hours, David was fighting for his life. He had a convulsion at 2:30 that morning and was rushed by ambulance to the hospital. It was determined that he had a brain tumor and needed immediate brain surgery. As a result of the convulsions David had also damaged his shoulders and needed surgery and continuing therapy. Although the tumor was diagnosed as benign, blood clots were to become another threat during the recovery period. That month the prototype cell experienced the reality of all they had learned as they moved into community and mobilized the church in ministry to the Hayes family. David and Connie together being apprentices in a couples cell was not to be, at least not for a while. Back to the prayer room and drawing board!

Public Enemy #1 - Cancer

As noted above, it was hoped that Nancy and Rebekah would bond and that out of the prototype would develop a youth girl's cell. The bonding did not take place and the youth cell was not to be, at least not when the prototype multiplied. Sometimes only in retrospect can one understand the moves of God. Had that bonding worked and a cell developed, it would not have survived the onslaught of what was to come.

Eric Stabinski, twenty-one year old son of Nancy and Mark Stabinski, had been getting progressively more ill as September went on. On September 15th Eric underwent a ninety minute biopsy procedure at

Mountainside Hospital. Surgeons attempted to identify a massive growth within the left side of Eric's chest cavity. The size of the growth was larger than what the biopsy surgical team had anticipated. In addition, the once believed singular core of growth seemed to have evolved into the creation of several smaller growths in close proximity to the original site. Eric was transferred to the Sloan-Kettering Cancer Center in New York City. The oncology team at Sloan-Kettering concluded that Eric had stage 3 aggressive and diffuse large b-cell lymphoma. Based upon the gravity of this diagnosis, treatments would begin with the first of eight, 21-day cycles of intensive chemotherapy. In addition, Eric would be enrolled as a candidate in the Phase III level clinical trial involving stem cell transplantation and full-body radiotherapy.

September through November were an intensive time for the Stabinski family. Eric's condition propelled the cell Nancy was a member in to the community stage. They have both supported the family and mobilized the church in ministry to Eric, Mark, Nancy, and Adam, the youngest son. In the providence of God, Nancy was freed from the responsibilities of cell leadership and placed as a member in a cell where she and her family could find encouragement and ministry.

AND IT CAME TO PASS...

Again, I want to emphasize that the cell church is a biotic organism. When viewed from the static pole it does possess an organizational dimension. There are things we can actually do to stimulate the release of the Spirit's activity. We can remove blockages. We can prepare the soil and plant the seed. We can water the soil with our prayers. However, we can neither create growth nor dictate how growth and development must happen. We must not forget to view the cell church from the dynamic pole also and recognize the work of the Spirit, who works all things after the counsel of His own will and places each one in the Body just as He desires, distributing to each one gifts and ministry in accordance with His will and purpose. Our job becomes one of listening and hearing the Lord the best we can, while from our failures learning better how to hear. Career changes do not surprise the Lord. Brain tumors do not thwart His plans. Cancer is not a threat to the work of His Kingdom. Our God reigns in the heavens above and on the earth below. "So, what was the final outcome?" you ask.

Women of Faith

A woman's cell was launched, meeting Tuesday evenings. Amelia agreed to lead the cell. She began with four apprentices–Ellen, Connie, Leigh, and Sonia. Even though she had not first experienced cell life, Sonia was asked to become an apprentice, knowing that with four apprentices in place, she probably would not be tapped to lead a cell when Amelia's cell multiplied in May. Connie could be given a similar experience, especially in light of David's recovery period. In the beginning we had believed for a woman's cell. In the end God provided a woman's cell.

An Unexpected Men's Cell

Mike Jetton wound up beginning a men's cell meeting on Wednesday evenings. RCC's leadership team from the beginning desired to launch a gender specific cell for men. However, when Mike was approached with the proposition, he nixed the idea. His desire was to lead a mixed adult cell. So how did a men's cell come about? In forming the cells, the leaders and apprentices along with the time and day of their cell was made known to the graduates from both Boot Camps. Each one was to let Twyla know of their desires. She in turn kept a master sign up list. As it turned out, the only ones who signed up for Mike's cell were men. He had no ladies or couples request his cell. When presented with that scenario that he had a nearly full cell of men who chose him, he agreed to lead a men's cell! Mike launched his cell with two interns–Alain and Joe. Alain was not a church member, but again an individual with untapped potential and another recent graduate of Boot Camp II. Joe, as you will recall, was not a church member either. Joe and Ellen had decided that although both agreed to become apprentices, they preferred to be in gender specific cells on different nights so they could trade off on child care. David Hayes and Bob Whipple also both became members of this men's cell, although not as apprentices.

An Adult Cell with an International Flavor

Roland and Naomi Urgino launched a mixed adult cell which meets on Friday evenings. This cell has two single women who opted for Friday over Tuesday because of school schedules. Although single, Ed III desired to be a part of a mixed adult as opposed to a gender specific men's cell. The cell has a Korean couple, Joshua and Jeannie Lee, graduates of Alliance Theological Seminary, who desire to eventually be sent overseas as cell church planters with the C&MA. They were also asked to become apprentices in addition to Ed III and Andy. Andy's wife, Kathy, opted to become a member of the Tuesday women's cell.

An Adult Cell in Crisis

The fourth cell launched was also a mixed adult cell. Ed and Debbie Woodward co-lead along with Paul and Mary Kadlub. They have no interns. They were launched with three other couples, Nancy Stabinski, and Dottie Behan, forming a full cell.

It was soon after the launch in September that Nancy's son Eric was diagnosed with cancer. In late October, Dottie, a spry 89 year old senior, unexpectedly went home to be with the Lord. Once again the cell was called upon to minister and mobilize the church into ministry. Life happens. When it does, the strength and reality of community in a cell will be tested. This cell has responded well both in ministry and in using the occasions for outreach to family members in need of Christ.

What About the Youth?

RCC has no youth cell...yet. Rebekah Giffone opted to attempt to start a youth cell on her own among her Home School Association. As a result, there is still no youth cell on the horizon at this point in time at RCC.

Philippine Cells

Riverside has had a Philippine Growth Group. The couple leading that group is presently in Boot Camp. When they finish in December, they are planning to become part of an existing cell and be trained to eventually launch a Philippine cell.

LEARNING TO RELEASE THE "WHAT MIGHT HAVE BEEN"

What follows is a rudimentary and partial evaluation of the Boot Camp/Prototype process undertaken by Riverside Community Church. However, the examples supplied will hopefully stimulate the reader's thinking into considering the types of areas that should be considered when undertaking a normal evaluation. At the same time, the reader can profit from what RCC actually learned in the process.

Evaluating the Boot Camp/Prototype Process - Cell Perspective

Where was the Boot Camp/Prototype Process Strong?

Strength #1 - Knowledge Coupled with Experience. Boot Camp provided a cognitive knowledge base out of which the apprentices would be required to build and function later as cell leaders. The coupling of knowledge and hands-on exercises throughout Boot Camp strengthened the teaching and challenged a change in lifestyle. Especially in the prototype, areas in need of development became apparent to the apprentices themselves. The experiential aspect brought the teaching in both venues down to the practical and relevant level.

Strength #2 - Common Experiences. The change in paradigms placed the Growth Group Leadership back to zero. By having them participate in Boot Camp, they all were given common experiences and equal opportunities to succeed. They were also provided with a common ground of experience with all their future cell members who would be brought through Boot Camp. Had the leadership not experienced Boot Camp first, they would have found themselves "behind the eight ball" and possibly struggling with issues their cell members had already resolved through their own Boot Camp experience. It is one thing to describe a cell and a cell lifestyle. It is quite another to experience it. For cell to be replicated, it was essential that the life be experienced, not simply envisioned. This is the difference between growing cells from an actual prototype and growing cells from a vision. The error of attempting cells from an analytical prototype was by-passed.

Where was the Prototype Multiplication Process Weak?

Weakness #1 - Shortened Prototype Cell Life Cycle. One of the biggest areas of weakness manifested itself in the shortened prototype cell life cycle. A normal cell cycle at RCC would run six to nine months in length. The cell cycle for the prototype cell ran sixteen weeks, barely four months. While there were many reasons leading up to that shortened life cycle, in the end it still proved to be a weakness.

First, it did not give those involved the experience of a typical cell cycle, resulting in a feeling of time compression. Because of the compressed time frame, those who began their apprentice training did so still not having completed the basic equipping track. Normally, a cell member would have completed the basic equipping in RCC's Passport I before asked to become a cell apprentice. Apprentices would then be ready to begin the cell leader equipping materials in RCC's Cell Leader Passport. Had a full time cycle been prototyped, the prototype cell members would have fully experienced RCC's basic cell member equipping and been ready to disciple others. Due to the shortened prototype, those tapped as first generation cell leaders were forced to place the basic equipping on hold while working through the leadership training material. This set back their equipping and later necessitated them discipling others in the new cells while simultaneously progressing on their own as best as they could through material that should have been completed prior to leading a cell.

Second, the outreach time was compressed and the cell members found themselves unable to complete the evangelistic outreach stage. They transitioned into evangelism well within the time frame they had, but had barely built relationships and experienced oikos evangelism when it was time to multiply and lead their own cell.

Third, the compressed time catapulted the cell through the normal stages of cell development faster than normal and did not allow for them to work through changes in their own lifestyle in a graceful manner. Without exception, the members of both prototype cells chaffed against the compressed time frame.

Fourth, the shortened cell life cycle required the identification of cell apprentices very early in the process, not allowing sufficient time for proven ministry and for the cream to truly rise.

Weakness #2 - Time Lag Between Boot Camp I and Cell. Some of those who completed Boot Camp I did not participate in the prototype cells, but were later enfolded into the first generation cells. It has been observed that they have often forgotten what they learned in Boot Camp. There was no cell experience to continue their transformation process. The result can be likened to a rubber band that is stretched, but then snaps back to its old shape if not put to immediate use.

Weakness #3 - Over Promotion of Both Boot Camps. Some attendees felt compelled to attend. It also required more cells to be formed to accommodate the Boot Camp graduates than is either normal or advisable. It did not allow church members to become interested and open to cells at their own pace. Because of the over promotion, many of those who attended were late majority people who needed to see an actual working cell model, not simply hear about it again.

Evaluating the Boot Camp/Prototype Process - NCD Perspective

Where was the Boot Camp/Prototype Process Strong?

Energy Transformation - RCC's leadership did a good job of anticipating negative energy arising as a result of Boot Camp and redirecting that energy. Groundwork that was laid by the pastoral staff and Board decreased what would otherwise have been hostile energies regarding the closure of the Growth Groups and the mandatory nature of Boot Camp prior to entrance into a cell. Additionally, sources of untapped potential were identified and the people brought into the Boot Camp and prototype cell process. Individuals that would have been passed over instead are now either leading cells or serving as apprentices. The positive energy arising from the Boot Camp experience was channeled into the prototype cell.

Functionality - The prototype cells communicated visually to the church beyond expectations. This was in large part a result of the crisis with David Hayes. The church family as a whole was able to see a dramatic increase in the level of community being lived out. It was even noted by and commented on by friends and unsaved neighbors of the Hayes family. The two prototypes experienced a high level of edification. Progress along RCC's equipping track was consistent. The cell members experienced a level of personal prayer and outreach to the lost they had not experienced prior. It was only the shortened time frame that kept the prototype cells from reaching the expected level of functionality in regards to evangelism and equipping.

Multiplication - The dynamics of multiplication were indeed built into the prototype cells. The formal resource based equipping worked well, Twyla and myself meeting with the immediate future cell leaders weekly to review the cell apprentice training tapes. Debriefings following cell were held regularly and a pattern established. The hands-on exercises provided opportunities for skill development. All of that led to cell leaders who were ready to multiply and understood how to begin to work with and train their own interns.

Where was the Boot Camp/Prototype Process Weak?

Interdependence - While the long and short term impact of Boot Camp and the Prototype Cell were generally anticipated, the long term impact of the compressed time frame for the life of the prototype was not adequately addressed. It is having and will continue to have an effect on the leaders who are now leading cells while playing catch up with their discipleship material and lifestyle transition. In addition, the women's cell lost two apprentices. One of the apprentices resigned to head up the children's ministry. A second apprentice resigned due to time conflicts. Had the prototype continued for a longer period, the individual in question could have worked through the lifestyle changes necessary to balance their business, family, and cell.

Chapter 6 ☞ *Learning to Evaluate Biotically*

Symbiosis - Neither Boot Camp nor the initial prototypes entered into much of a symbiotic relationship with any other ministry of the church. At best, it can be said that those who were part of the Worship Ministry were released to lead in times of worship during the Boot Camp cycles. There were no worship personnel in the initial prototype cells. The Care Ministry and Bagel Ministry have yet to be brought alongside the Cell Ministry as suggested earlier, although progress in that direction is being made through RCC's NCD Implementation Team. Ways are also still being explored for ALPHA and the Cell Ministry to work together in evangelism.

Multi-usage - Again, this was a weak area of development in general. Having said that, plans are presently being made to video tape testimonies from Boot Camp graduates for use in future Boot Camp enlistments and the forms developed and skills realized through the prototypes are being utilized by the current crop of cell leaders in the training of their own apprentices.

While this has only been a rudimentary and partial evaluation of the Boot Camp/Prototype process undertaken by Riverside Community Church, if the reader has gained from what RCC actually learned in the process, and if the exercise has provided fertile soil in which the Lord has stimulated the reader's thinking regarding cell decisions and NCD principles, then we will count the exercise as profitable. What remains is to answer the simple question, "What is the next step?"

YOUR NEXT STEP

THE STEPS OF A MAN ARE ESTABLISHED BY THE LORD; AND HE DELIGHTS IN HIS WAY. PSALM 37:23

Chapter 7 ☛ Your Next Step

THE JOURNEY COMPLETED

In looking at the journey to come, it is sometimes helpful to look at the journey that has passed. What have you, the reader, received thus far?

Whether NCD proponent or cell church enthusiast, you have been given a bird's eye view of the main principles of NCD. You have seen that Natural Church Development is a paradigm – a way of thinking about church growth that takes into account quality (health) and not just quantity (numbers). In fact, NCD suggests that quality should take priority over quantity in church growth thinking. You have discovered afresh that Natural Church Development is also a long-term strategic process for progressively improving a church's health. It is not an "easy fix" for what ails a church. The strategy of Natural Church Development is built upon three building blocks. The eight quality characteristics together form the first building block. The six biotic principles unite to create the second building block. The third building block is the minimum strategy. It has been suggested throughout that the bipolar approach is essential for a theological understanding of church growth; and it is definitely the theological key for understanding what Natural Church Development is all about.

With the aforementioned as our common understanding, you were challenged to develop stereophonic cell edification. Edification in the cell and through the cell was thoroughly explained and illustrated. The bipolar grid was applied to the area of cell edification. Stereophonic edification was described in terms of a divine partnership between Jesus and His instruments of edification.

The problem of the two-winged bird flying with only one and one-half wings was next addressed. The author confronted both cell church reader and NCD reader with the need of developing a bipolar ecclesiology. The author contended that the current cell church paradigm is a far cry from the Church described by Paul to the Ephesian saints, seeming to be a church comprised of a head with interconnecting cells, rather than a head with a body. The deficiency of the cell/celebration paradigm was addressed and in its place an alternate gift-based paradigm was proposed, a paradigm illustrated by the human body with its interdependent body systems.

To bring the often theological down into the practical realm, Riverside Community Church in Nutley, New Jersey was used to illustrate how the principles of NCD could be easily and beneficially employed in a cell church context. The process of biotic thinking, planning, and evaluating was explained and illustrated by RCC's journey as it embraced the principles of NCD and sought to transition to a cell paradigm. A common cell church problem was addressed and good cell decisions improved with the assistance of NCD.

THE JOURNEY AHEAD - NEXT STEPS
SO, WHERE *DO* WE GO FROM HERE?

By this point the cell church reader has hopefully seen the challenge presented by NCD to be not a threat, but a blessing. Holistic small groups are good. They are vital. All that is done in and through them I trust is the work and ministry of the Church. However, all the work of the Church cannot be done within the context of any small group or cell, or even a system of interconnected cells that still has not formed a viable body life. Cells can do what cells can do. But a body can far outstrip even what the sum of its individual parts may be able to accomplish. NCD addresses the issues of healthy body life and growth. We in the cell church need that perspective. Where do *we* go from here? I would suggest we re-consider our ecclesiastical paradigm from a bipolar perspective. I would suggest we seek to master the principles of biotic growth and life even as we have sought to master the principles of cell church. I suggest we pursue learning to think and plan and evaluate biotically with as great vigor as we have pursued thinking and planning and evaluating from our cell perspective. In other words, I would suggest we embrace the principles of NCD as we have embraced the principles of cell for the greater glory of His Body!

To simply enjoin you, the NCD reader, to embrace the cell church paradigm seems a bit abrupt. Allow me to suggest that the cell church paradigm will provide a context and wineskin for answering problems that hitherto you have been unable to adequately answer. For example, as you consistently raise your minimum factors you will experience greater health and growth. You may tweak and fine tune your current paradigm in attempting even greater evangelism. However, referring once again to Joel Barker's paradigm research and curve shown on the following page, I would suggest to you that your present paradigm is at or nearing stage "C" and there is only so much more you can gain from continuing with life as is. The cell church paradigm offers a new paradigm for evangelism in the context of cells and corporate body ministry that provides answers to problems you are facing, but for which have no effective answers.

The Paradigm Curve

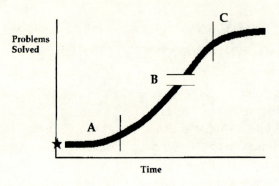

The same can be said for discipleship/equipping problems, leadership development and empowering problems, and the ever present problem of mobilizing the 80% of your membership who does 20% of the work and somehow always leaves 80% of the work of ministry to the other 20% of your members. May I suggest your next step is to thoughtfully and thoroughly consider moving to a cell church paradigm, without abandoning that which you have already gained through great pain and effort.

We come now full circle to the scripture with which we began this journey. At the end of the day, David still sums it up best in Psalm 133. Where there is unity, there is the blessing of God.

Natural Church Development and Cell Church - Friends or Foes? I would hate to miss a blessing from God because I was blind to a friendship and unity He desired to create!

Behold, how good and how pleasant it is
For brothers to dwell together in unity!

It is like the precious oil upon the head,
Coming down upon the beard,
Even Aaron's beard,
Coming down upon the edge of his robes.

It is like the dew of Hermon
Coming down upon the mountains of Zion;
For there the LORD commanded the blessing—
life forever.

WORKS CITED

Barker, Joel A. Future Edge. New York: William Morrow and Company, 1992.

Boren, M. Scott. Making Cell Groups Work. Houston: Cell Group Resources, 2002.

Brickman, Leslie. Preparing the 21st Century Church. Carol Stream: ChurchSmart Resources, 1996.

Comiskey, Joel. How to Lead a Great Cell Group Meeting. Houston: Cell Group Resources, 2002.

Etienne, Wouehi Louan. Personal interview. 10 August 2000.

Logan, Robert. Releasing You Church's Potential. Carol Stream: ChurchSmart Resources, 1998.

---. Cell Church Planters Guide. Carol Stream: ChurchSmart Resources, 2001.

Robert, Yaye Dion. Personal interview. 9-11 August 2000.

Schwarz, Christian A. Natural Church Development. Carol Stream: ChurchSmart Resources, 1996.

---. Paradigm Shift in the Church. Carol Stream: ChurchSmart Resources, 1999.

ADDITIONAL RESOURCES
by Les Brickman

PREPARING THE 21ST CENTURY CHURCH

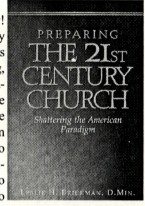

Phenomenal power! Explosive growth! Genuine community! Can the church in America, twenty-one centuries later, really experience what we read about in the Book of Acts? Les Brickman shows you why the answer is a resounding, "Yes...if". Whether a church planter just beginning, a seasoned pastor, or a church leader, you will be challenged to the core both by the questions and answers you discover. Are you willing to spend the necessary time to prepare a wineskin able to release your vision from God? Are you prepared to pay the price so you can embrace His destiny for your ministry and church? Journey with Dr. Brickman and come to understand what values, lifestyle, and activities will have to change for you to experience what they experienced, and beyond. "How to" books on church growth and cell ministry too often miss the critical preparation so vital to releasing God's life through the Church. Informative and theological, yet practical and prophetic, Preparing the 21st Century Church will cause you to reconsider the whole way you "do church", even "cell church". **Order Online: www.strategiccell.com**

SPIRITUAL GIFTS IN THE CELL CHURCH

In this series Dr. Brickman covers the basics of manifestational and functional spiritual gifts, including how to release them both in the cell and in the corporate congregation. This series also includes a practical implementation plan to move your church forward into a gift-based ministry, moving beyond the prevalent but ineffective volunteer based or shared ministry based systems of ministry. Syllabus notes provide a great supplement to the tape series. Eight audio cassettes in album.75+ page syllabus in 3-ring notebook. **Order Online: www.strategiccell.com**

Needing Additional Cell Church Training Resources?
We Have What You Need!

Strategic Cell Ministries International
www.strategiccell.com

WHEN BOOKS & TAPES ARE NOT ENOUGH!

CUSTOMIZED CELL CHURCH CONSULTATION

- ☞ Detailed and customized assessments and recommendations concerning your particular cell church's needs, problems and plans

- ☞ Assistance by phone, e-mail, or in person, as you learn to develop and implement your comprehensive transition plans

- ☞ Customized cell material developed specifically to fit you and your cells' unique needs along with leadership training seminars tailor made to fit your cell leadership team and church leadership needs – One size DOES NOT fit all!

NATURAL CHURCH DEVELOPMENT (NCD) COACHING

- ✔ SCMI provides NCD coaching to help your leaders learn how to create the environment and to implement the biotic principles vital to releasing "all by itself" natural growth within your church.

- ✔ What is the role of an NCD coach? NCD coaches are...
    - ❐ **Familiar** with the whole approach of NCD and all of the available tools, including the theological background.
    - ❐ **Trained** in coaching techniques.
    - ❐ **Licensed** and supported by the National NCD Partner.
    - ❐ **Experienced** in bridging the gap between the universal principles that NCD describes, and the sometimes complicated situations in a local church.

- ✔ Our primary primary job is to ask the right questions to help you and your church leadership discover creative answers.

TRANSFORMATIONAL LEADERSHIP COACHING
– Building Leaders from the Inside Out –

Experience the Transformation of Personal Coaching

- **A Professional TLC Coach is a Personal Change Agent**
  Coaches help people like you grow faster, perform at a higher level, understand themselves more deeply, and live with greater purpose and fulfillment. Professionally trained in a unique set of leadership skills, coaches help you identify important goals and priorities, strategize about how to reach them, and overcome obstacles that crop up along the way. In the same way that a personal trainer helps a pro athlete maximize performance, a personal coach can help you get the most out of life.

- **Coaching is a Transformational Conversation**
  The biggest surprise for first-time clients is realizing that the coach isn't there to give advice. Instead, powerful, incisive coaching questions stimulate you to examine the things in life that matter most from new angles. A coaching conversation can transform the way you look at life.

- **Coaching is a Transparent Relationship**
  A coach is a friend and confidant, your greatest supporter, and someone who knows you well enough to call out the best in you. A transparent relationship with your coach frees you to go to places you've never gone before.

- **Coaching is a Support System for Change**
  With support, encouragement and accountability from someone who believes in you, you can do far more than you could ever accomplish alone. A coach helps you stay on track, overcome obstacles, and convert your want-to into concrete steps that get in your date book and get done.

- **Coaching is Continuous Leadership Development**
  Coaches don't give solutions: they help you solve your problems. Coaching is helping you learn instead of telling you what to do. By leveraging every situation to build your capacity as a leader and a person, coaching prepares you to conquer much bigger challenges in the future.

- A **Personal Coach** can help you reach your goals and lead a more satisfying, purposeful life. So if you want more from life—more growth, greater purpose, maximum performance–a personal coach might just be your key!

UNLEASH THE POWER OF COACHING IN YOUR ORGANIZATION - *ACT*

- **ACT – Real Training for Real Coaches**
  This **A**ccelerated **C**oach **T**raining program is designed for those who want to coach a few people at a time or coach in a volunteer role. Designed around the same exercises, role plays and one-on-one coaching approach we use to train professional coaches, the ACT program offers the kind of serious training that gets lasting results, but within an accessible time frame. We'll have a group of your leaders coaching effectively in only 9 weeks, then follow up with 12 more weeks of ongoing support to get them off to a great start.

- **The ACT Program is Perfect for:**
  - Small group leaders/overseers
  - Church or parachurch staff
  - Ministry team leaders
  - Businessmen or managers
  - Anyone who wants to coach!

- **When you enroll in the ACT program, you'll receive:**
  - Two fun, interactive skills workshops.
  - Four coaching sessions with a professional coach.
  - 14 tele-class skill sessions.
  - A great learning relationship with a peer partner.
  - A 100-page manual full of coaching resources.
  - Eight input sessions on CD.
  - Membership in the TLC coaching community.
  - Training that can apply toward a professional coaching certification.

Strategic Cell Ministries International
www.strategiccell.com

Printed in the United States
47182LVS00003B/66